I climbed Kilimanjaro-
and learnt things.
(And if I DID YOU CAN)

By Philip Crompton

I climbed Kilimanjaro- and learnt things.

This book was first published in Great Britain in paperback during April 2024.

The moral right of Philip Crompton is to be identified as the author of this work and has been asserted by him in accordance with the Copyright, Designs and Patents Act of 1988.

All rights are reserved, and no part of this book may be produced or utilized in any format, or by any means, electronic or mechanical, including photocopying, recording or by any information storage or retrieval system, without prior permission in writing from the publishers - Four Winds

All rights reserved.

ISBN: 979-8884853539

Copyright © April 2024 Philip Crompton

I climbed Kilimanjaro -

and learnt things.

(And if I DID YOU CAN)

Who should read this book ?

This book is aimed at **anyone** who really wants to fulfil their potential. Young people who are wondering what life might hold will find it helpful. Older people will find it encouraging too. Life always has opportunities even if they are not yet visible. Sometimes you must look through the mist to see what is out there.

The pages that follow combine three recent projects that I have found deeply satisfying:

- My ascent of Mount Kilimanjaro in 2023
- The "I DID YOU CAN" podcast series of 2022.
- The 2019 publication "In Search of My Alumni".

Each project involved exploring what it means to fulfil your potential and become the person you want to be.

"In Search of My Alumni" opened the door. By travelling around England and conversing with people who were at school in the period when I was leading schools, I realised that so many had not yet acquired the skills and experiences needed to live the life they dreamt of. I concluded that if they relied upon their years in school to show them the way they just might be disappointed.

"I DID YOU CAN" involved interviews with 50 people who have lived very different, but ultimately satisfying, lives. It explores their backgrounds, their youthful aspirations, and the obstacles they have faced to get where they are. There are lessons to be learnt for us all.

As I climbed Mount Kilimanjaro, I realised that so many people had the physical and mental abilities required to meet such a challenge, but perhaps they didn't yet know it. Similarly, so many have the skills, talent and personality traits needed to live their best lives but, again, they are not fully aware of it. The climb and the aftermath led me to identify 8 lessons which, if absorbed and acted upon, should lead to greater satisfaction in life.

I believe people of all ages and backgrounds can benefit from the lessons learnt from the adventure.

Some opening words

"Mount Kilimanjaro is Africa's tallest mountain at 5,895 metres (19,340 feet). It is the largest free-standing mountain in the world. It is a volcano though geologists say it has not erupted for 360,000 years. In 1889, the German geographer Hans Meyer and Austrian mountaineer Ludwig Purtscheller became the first people on record to reach the summit of Kilimanjaro. Kilimanjaro has since become a popular climb. Because mountaineering gear and experience is not needed to reach the peak, tens of thousands of climbers ascend the mountain each year. The climb is still dangerous, however, because of the risk of altitude sickness—a condition climbers experience if they ascend too quickly, which can be deadly if not treated right."

https://education.nationalgeographic.org/resource/kilimanjaro/

I knew a bit about the highest mountain in Africa. But not much. I just thought that, at 63 years of age, it presented a challenge that I ought to embrace. Climbing Mount Kilimanjaro turned out to be one of the most memorable experiences of my life and a way bigger achievement than I had anticipated. The adventure had so many sides to it- laughter, exhaustion, doubt, sadness, inspiration, conversation, exertion, weariness, and learning. Quite the trip. I just had to write it up in the hope that it would encourage others to have a go.

There are two parts to this book. The first section aims to capture the atmosphere of the climb itself: the staging posts, equipment, personalities of my climbing companions, the organisation of the support team, the food, the scenery, and the discomfort. Hopefully the account will persuade waverers to give it a go. At this early stage, let's be clear. It is doable. Some don't get to the top, but many do. I was in my 60's, had been doing a bit of jogging and dog walking yet managed to get to the top. My podcast series is called **"I DID YOU CAN"**. Keep that thought with you. I do not try to pretend that I have any special talent. Quite the reverse. Many people will join the queue of those willing to back this up!

Writing the record of the climb itself is the easy bit. We climbed, and here is what I noted and remembered. I was always going to record that bit. Straightforward enough. The second part crept up on me. Climbing a mountain like Kilimanjaro has so many lessons for life. I learned a lot about myself as I strolled, struggled, sympathised, and smiled my way up and down the slopes. Most of my learning was revision. It wasn't new, it was re-enforced. Information that I had absorbed over the years. Some of it was a development of something I knew. A bit of it was eye opening. Completely fresh information that hadn't previously occurred to me.

When I reflected upon the learning, I was hit by a little sadness that it had taken me 63 years to gather it together. If only I had known all this when I was younger. How many times has that sentiment been shared throughout human history? *"If only I knew then what I know now".*

I will ensure that I make good use of what I thought about on Kilimanjaro but if I had been able to take it on board when I was in my teens or twenties then who knows how life might have worked out? What colour might it have added to life? Which places might it have taken me to? What extra confidence might I have had? Could I have understood others better? How might I have done my job better? Would I have had a different job? Could I have been a better dad? A better partner? Who knows? As the Irishman Paul Brady sang in one of my favourite songs *"The answer is nobody knows"*

Imagine though if, to the backdrop of Mount Kilimanjaro, I could pass on just some of these life lessons to people making their way in the world. The second part of the book is my attempt to do just that. As you read the first section you'll see signposts to key parts of the second section. I hope they help.

Let's start the climb.

Section 1
The ascent of Kilimanjaro: February 2023

Why ?

On my 55th birthday in 2014, I had put together a travel bucket list of sorts. I had done a reasonable amount of travelling I suppose. Nothing too adventurous. Most of the British Isles, a lot of Europe, a few parts of the U.S.A. There was a lot still to see and the clock was ticking quite loudly. On my list I scribbled down the Great Wall of China, Tokyo, India, St. James' Park in Newcastle, Hanoi, the Northern Lights, Haydock Park Racecourse, Nashville, Havana, the Grand Canyon, Wimbledon - and Mount Kilimanjaro.

Kilimanjaro. It's a great name, don't you think? I didn't really know much about it when I created my list. I was fully aware that it was in East Africa. Tanzania or Kenya? I wasn't completely sure. (It's Tanzania). "The Snows of Kilimanjaro" by Ernest Hemingway was a famous short story. Hands up. I hadn't read it. I have now. The mountain in "The Lion King" that soared up above the Serengeti Plain. As a geography teacher, I'd often used it to illustrate the way temperatures dropped with height. Snow on the Equator? How's that possible? There was no denying that Kilimanjaro existed nor that it was spectacular. And now I'd expressed an interest in visiting it.

The opportunity

I'd known Ian Marron for 5 years or so. Our paths had crossed several times and we'd had a few brief chats. We became better acquainted through Milo and Ivy. I had acquired Milo, a golden Cocker Spaniel, in January 2021 and Ian's wife Jo had been given Ivy– a black and female version of Milo - as a birthday present around the same time. Ian was allowed to take Ivy for walks, and we met up in the Charnwood area of Leicestershire for regular woodland wanders with stops for coffee. It was all very pleasant. Ian and I got to know each other better and it became obvious that we had a shared interest in travel and less of an interest in work. Ian had worked in the corporate world until his mid 50's before opting out and throwing himself into voluntary activity, dog walking - and travel. I had led schools for 20 years before leaving that behind me in 2018, just before my 60th birthday, to explore portfolio living. I envisaged a balance between part time employment, writing, cycling, running, family life- and travel.

As Ian and I chatted and attempted to train 2 hyperactive spaniels, we lightly discussed the possibility of a shared trip. Ian had travelled extensively in his working life and since finishing had spent time in Canada, Peru and Vietnam. My working life hadn't allowed quite so much travel but after 2018, I had cycled in India, Vietnam, and southern France. The COVID-19 pandemic had held up everything. There was a travel hiatus. Along with what seemed like 50% of the over 50's in the UK, I had bought a campervan and toured eastern France with Anne in the spring of 2022. That toe in the water had led me to ponder a return to something a little further afield. Cycling Costa Rica had a certain appeal.

I knew that Ian's son and daughter-in-law, following their marriage, had taken an extended break from their work with Adidas to travel the world. It all sounded so exciting and modern. When Anne and I were married our honeymoon consisted of three days in Shropshire! A far cry from Brazil, Argentina, South Africa, Uganda – and Kilimanjaro.

It was early July 2022 when Ian contacted me to say that Daniel and Emma, the couple in question, had signed up for an ascent of Kilimanjaro in February of 2023. There were apparently 2 vacancies on their trip, and they wondered if he fancied joining them. And he thought I might be interested in the final place. Costa Rica on the bike or climbing the tallest mountain in Africa? One sounded warm and relaxing. The other said cold and stressful. I had a quick chat with Anne who, I must add, was still working and had little interest in long haul adventures. She said "It sounds like a great opportunity ". She didn't say " Wow, does that mean you'll be out from under my feet for a few weeks?" but I suspect it had occurred to her.

"Yes. I'm up for it, Ian" I informed him.

"Great. You don't need to do anything for now. I'll pay the deposit. We'll need to pay the rest in December. And we leave on February 2nd " he replied.

February was ages hence. So, I closed my mind to what awaited.

My mountain climbing CV.

At my daughter Cat's graduation from Lancaster University, I had been inspired by the Chancellor, one Sir Christopher Bonnington. What a remarkable life he has had. 19 Himalayan expeditions, climbs of K2, Annapurna, and The Old Man of Hoy. And in 1985, he became the oldest man, at 50, to get to the summit of Mount Everest. An extraordinary mountaineer. I am no Chris Bonnington.

My conquests have been modest but more demanding than some, I guess.

I had twice conquered the highest mountain in Great Britain, Ben Nevis (1345m). The first time was when I was 17, with my family. It had felt painless as a teenager. Presumably it wasn't but I've eliminated any discomfort from my memory. I recall my dad saying he needed to stay at sea level with our aging Labrador. Harry would have been 47, I think. He was far happier staying down below with his 'Daily Mirror' and a cup of tea. The second time was with Anne. We'd booked a few days near Fort William to acknowledge our 25th wedding anniversary. The weather was glorious. Naively, we joined the queues climbing the highest mountain in the UK on the hottest day of the year. I wore jeans! Bonkers. It was a tough day, but the views were wonderful. I remember being thrilled to soak my feet in the stream near the car park when we made it back at around 4.30pm.

Scafell Pike (978m) had been straight forward enough. The last hour was a bit of a drag as I hopped from rock to rock and the mist that shrouded the summit meant there wasn't much to be seen. But hey, the highest mountain in England was ticked off the list in 2001.

Snowdon, or Yr Wyddfa (1085m), had been conquered just the once. I had cycled north from Nottingham, to visit my old university friends David and Margaret in Colwyn Bay. I'd stopped off at a Bed and Breakfast at Bangor-on-Dee near Wrexham, failing to appreciate just how many hills remained if I was to complete the journey. I was weary when I met Anne in Rhos-on-Sea and relieved to have a relaxing night with our friends. The two of us had committed to take on the challenge of ascending Snowdon on the August Bank Holiday. We had parked in Llanberis and, despite my over used legs feeling the strain of a long cycle ride, the trek to the summit was not over-taxing. The presence of the steam train was a bit odd. Casual visitors hop on, have a stroll around the visitor centre and then roll back down. It does distort the sense of adventure a little. We distorted it even more by choosing to descend by a different route – I think it was called the Ranger path. It seemed so logical. "Let's vary it a bit" we'd agreed. We reached the main(ish) road, turned right, and started to walk. 30 minutes later we were getting suspicious and tired. After 50 minutes we were nervous and very tired. We called at a camp site and asked how far it was to Llanberis.

"About 12 miles," said the humourless receptionist. After a quick conflab we returned to the desk and asked if there was local taxi company that we could contact.

"The nearest one is in Llanberis. And it's a Bank Holiday," said our reluctant friend. Knowing there was no phone signal I asked if we could use her landline. 40 minutes later a cab arrived. After another 40 minutes we were back in Llanberis £40 worse off than we had been when we set off.

I've always liked looking at mountains and being surrounded by them. My daughters are capable skiers and enjoy the rush of sliding down steep slopes. I am not a good skier- in fact I'm hopeless - and find anything beyond a Blue slope terrifying. To the uninitiated a Black slope is vertical, a Red slope nearly vertical, a Blue slope gentler and a Green one is almost flat. I put it down to delaying my debut on the piste until I was 50 and being far too aware of what might go wrong when you are moving at speed down an icy slope. Especially when you are 6 feet 2 and the wrong side of 14 stones. I was reassured to hear that the risks on Kilimanjaro were not really steep slope related.

It's fair to say that my experience on the higher parts of our planet is not comparable to that of Sir Chris Bonnington. It is important that you understand your capabilities when you set challenges, but my 50 plus interviews for the **"I DID YOU CAN"** podcast series illustrate that you need to take time to know yourself. And that's one of the pieces of learning that was strengthened by the climb of Kilimanjaro.

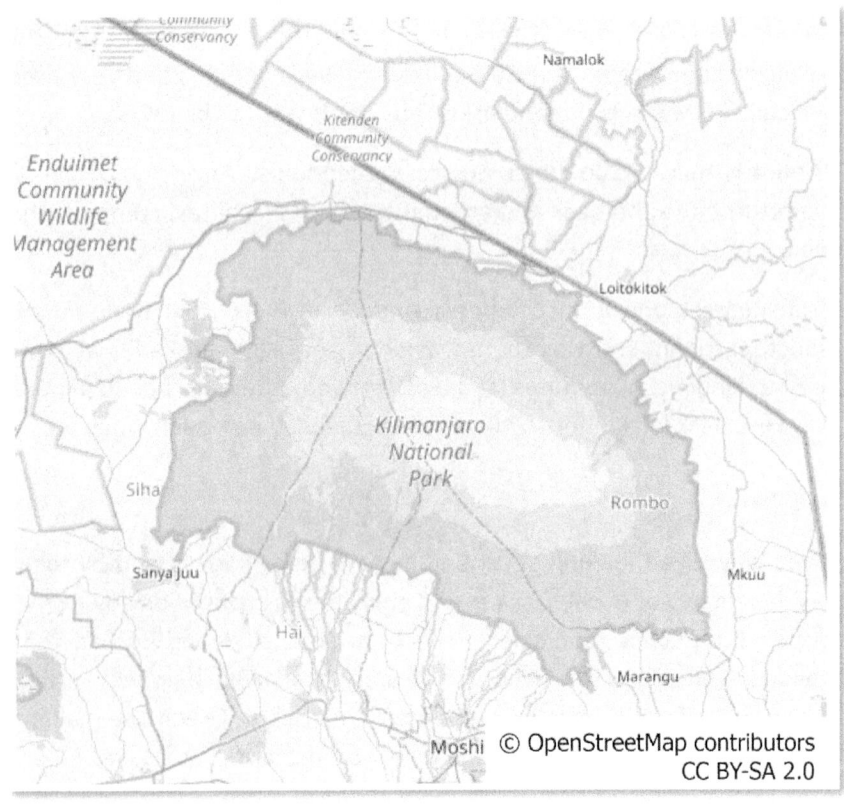

Preparing

In August, I had been walking in the fields near to my home in the Nottinghamshire countryside and met up with Margaret and Ken, who lived in the same village as me. The conversation went from a polite "How are you?" and "What a lovely morning?" to "Oh my goodness, I'm going to climb Kilimanjaro too". Yes, in Margaret I'd found a fellow traveller. She was all set to attempt to get to the top of the mountain. Margaret was well advanced in her preparation. In the previous few months, she had climbed Ben Nevis and also reached the top of Snowdon by setting off at midnight and slowly, slowly reaching the top by dawn. She explained that Snowdon was supposed to replicate the final stage of Kilimanjaro and was considered to be good preparation for the nocturnal push to the top that was a key part of any attempt on the African giant. Margaret had been training for weeks and had started to collect sponsorship. I wished her well.

Ian and I discussed what Margaret had told me and considered whether we should follow a similar programme. We talked about a trip to the Lake District, regular visits to the nearby Peak District and walks up Beacon Hill in Leicestershire (248m). But then we compared our current levels of fitness. I did the local parkrun (5km) every week and had a couple of practice sessions on Tuesdays and Thursdays. Ian walked the dog a lot and had once been a highly rated 800m runner, coming desperately close to representing Ireland in the 1984 Olympics and being a pace setter for the 1980's superstar, and now commentator, Steve Cram. Despite the glory days being over 30 years earlier he remained sure his core fitness would be sufficient to deal with our Kilimanjaro challenge. I thought I should increase my work a bit, so I committed to run the Lancaster half marathon in October and planned a visit to the less than wild uplands of Shropshire with Milo and the campervan.

All would be well Ian assured me. To back this up he referred to some 'research' that said if you could run 5km on 4 consecutive days you would be able to deal with the exertion needed to scale Kilimanjaro.

The next time I saw Margaret she sadly had to tell me that she had hurt her foot and was forced to pull out of the trip 3 weeks before departure. She was clearly upset by this. I do hope she has another go. Anyone who has walked slowly up Mount Snowdon in darkness deserves to have the African experience.

I did visit Shropshire. I stayed at a camp site just outside Church Stretton for 2 days and climbed to the top of Caer Caradoc (402m) on a windy October morning. Wonderful views but my map reading skills proved to be rusty and I took a couple of wrong turns. Poor Milo then had to wander beside me for 12 miles before we got back to the van. He still accompanied me to the pub that evening.

The parkrun and the practice sessions with 11 similarly aged and retired buddies continued to play a big part in my life. Was it the running or the coffee and chat that made it so important? It might be worth clarifying what parkrun is. Every Saturday morning at 9.00am, people of all ages and abilities assemble at parks across the UK to run 5 kilometres. I'm sure there must be something that has increased the fitness of the population more than parkrun but I'm struggling to think of one. Banning smoking in public places perhaps? I had been taking part for 4 years and even though I'd gone from being the quickest (or least slow) member of our happy band of 7 to the 5th quickest (at best) following the recruitment of 4 slimline speedsters, I continued to turn up and push myself. One of the group, another Ian, had done a bit of mountaineering and asked if I knew how hard Kili was.

"Oh yeah. Course I do" I fibbed.

"What training are you doing?" he asked.

"Well, parkruns. Oh, and I went to Shropshire" I replied. Ian didn't reply. And that was troubling.

The Lancaster half marathon haunted me. It had been in my diary for a couple of months, and I had done a few longer runs to get my system in shape, but the word "jog" would be an exaggeration of the velocity of my efforts. As the date approached, I checked the weather app on my phone and saw that heavy rain was forecast. I spied an excuse. But by the day before the event, it was evident that the weather was not going to be a barrier. A couple of showers, a bit breezy, grey sky. I had to do it. So, I stood at the start line in Morecambe surrounded by skinny people in vests and managed to get round in 1 hour 56 minutes. "Slower than I used to do but hey I'm 63. I'm Kili fit!" I told myself. As I drove home my legs seized up and I needed to stretch at Charnock Richard Services by the side the M6 but that was normal after a 13-mile run. I was pleased with myself. That's always a dangerous place to be.

The crisis of confidence

I often wake in the middle of the night and struggle to get back to sleep. It is very frustrating and the more annoying it becomes the more difficult it is to fix. Everyone knows that a slight niggle can become a huge worry when focussed upon at 4.00am. And so, it was with Project Kilimanjaro.

The balance for the trip had to be paid in early December and it was a significant amount of money. I had already paid £800 for the return flight from Heathrow to Nairobi, £110 for the travel insurance and another £2000 was due soon. When I woke early on Friday morning, my mind quickly became scrambled. Was I fit enough? Was I too old? Did older people struggle? Was it a waste of money? Could I claim the cost of the flight back? Would the altitude be too much? So much to worry about.

I got out of bed, went to another room to access my phone, and spent an hour accessing articles and YouTube clips about Kilimanjaro. Why I didn't do that in July is anyone's guess. The information made me increasingly anxious. I didn't get back to sleep. Altitude was a big concern. The internet had many stories of people of all ages who had been taken ill on the mountain. Some had been helicoptered to hospital, a few had died. There were scare stories about the number of casualties being massaged by the Tanzanian authorities because it was such an important money spinner and the last thing, they wanted was for people to be put off by the risks. I spotted a story of an 83-year-old woman climbing the mountain but then it turned out that she was a lifelong mountaineer so maybe it wasn't such a big deal. The companies selling the packages were keen to say that age made little difference. Older people (that seemed to be the over 40's, I noticed) tended to be more sensible and approached the climb with respect by going very slowly and giving the body time to adjust to the reducing amount of oxygen in the air. Or so the publicity packs assured me.

The video clips and stories about Summit Day presented a vision of hell. "The toughest day of my life", said one young woman who, upon reflection, was about 23 and maybe hadn't faced too many physical challenges. "So pleased it was over", said a fit looking chap in his 30's. I looked at pictures of those who made it smiling and waving at the camera but then saw an article that told me 30% of participants didn't get to the top. That seemed an awfully big number.

At 6.00am, I was a spent force. I messaged Ian:

"Been looking into what going up Kili involves. Sorry. I don't think I can do it."

Later, my daughter Maire was to express surprise that I'd ever felt so unsure of myself. But I did. It seemed highly unlikely that I would be on the plane at the start of February.

Ian drove out to talk it through. He told me not to feel that I would be letting him down. He was sure that one of his daughters would take the place. It seemed that it was the "Last Chance Saloon" when he suggested that I speak to a friend of his who had completed the climb 5 years earlier. I spoke to Carol for half an hour the next day. She was in the same age group, hadn't done much preparation and described the climb as "a strenuous, but not dangerous, long walk". The Summit Day it seemed had been very difficult but when I told her what I did in a typical week she felt sure I would be fine. However, she stressed that the effect of altitude was unpredictable. Apparently the fittest of people found themselves struggling with headaches and vomiting. You just didn't know. She suggested I consider taking Diamox because that was known to help. As Carol was a GP, I listened carefully and slowly changed my view. I could do it. Get the mindset right and I would have a good chance of surviving the experience. And I didn't want to waste the best part of £1000 that I'd already spent. The darkness had gone, the sun was shining. Bring it on.

> **Life lesson 1: Know yourself**
>
> *" A genius in a wrong position could look like a fool "*
>
> Idowu Koyenikan.
>
> More to follow.....

Paid the money – so start thinking.

G Adventures, the highly recommended, Toronto-based company that our trip was booked through, had sent a list of equipment that we would need to have along with an itinerary. There was an obvious packing dilemma. A backpack has its limitations. I was puzzled by the expectation that I would have the clothing required to ensure I would be comfortable at sea level, where the temperature was sure to be 30 degrees centigrade or more, whilst also carrying the right gear to protect me at much higher levels where temperatures were often well below freezing and the risk of snow, hail and driving rain was relatively high.

I was reassured by the fact that we would visit a rental shop before we set off and could hire anything we didn't have but still made a call to G Adventures to check out a few things. The sleeping bag was a big one. Yes, '4 seasons' sleeping bags were available for hire at $40 as were fleece tops, thermal underwear, poles, gloves and hats. Fleece jackets were described as "essential" in the information pack and couldn't be hired. It was the same with boots. I already had decent boots, ski gloves, a woolly hat, and a thick fleece that my daughter had bought me for Christmas. After an evening's research, I bought a down jacket for £200. I was assured that it would be effective at very low temperatures and when it arrived, I was delighted to see how small it was when packed away. I would also need to take shorts and T shirts. What I wore on the last bit of the climb turned out to be an important issue.

In January, Anne and I had booked a week in Fuerteventura in the Canary Islands. There was a cheap flight from East Midlands Airport and with the help of an Airbnb in Corralejo, and despite the mixed weather, we had a relaxing break. The experience ranged from lying on a beach watching surfers in El Cortillo to trekking up and down the volcanoes that covered the island. The Martian landscape was ideal for experiencing the wonders of volcanic climbs. They weren't anywhere near as big as Kilimanjaro. The highest point is Pico de la Zarza and that is only 800m. I didn't venture far enough south to reach such heights.

One morning whilst Anne was at a beachside yoga session, I went for a run across the cinder strewn path that led to one of the volcanoes close to Corralejo. Sadly, I lost concentration, tripped, and managed to end up with cuts and scrapes on my chin, hands and knees. The return through the town centre attracted sympathetic glances from locals who were probably thinking "Oh dear, that elderly gentleman shouldn't be out running on his own. I hope he never tries to climb a major African volcano. That would be silly".

In the days that followed my ascent of the mountain, I pondered how I might have prepared better. To have done no preparation at all would have been foolhardy. I could have done more. Spending some time at a high altitude was the obvious omission but arranging it would have been a serious stretch. There is little doubt that any challenge needs thinking through beforehand. And so, my second piece of learning from Kilimanjaro is.......

Life lesson 2: Prepare well

"Prepare to go. Before anything else preparation is the key to success"

Alexander Graham Bell

It's time to go.

Ian had been talking about taking the train to London, meeting a friend for an afternoon, and staying with his daughter before heading to Heathrow. It seemed like a decent plan until it became clear that strikes by the rail unions were going to make it very risky. So, I collected Ian from his home in Quorn in Leicestershire at 4.30am on Thursday February 2nd. His formidable backpack was slung into the boot, and we drove to Heathrow Airport's Terminal 5 car park. The Meet and Greet set up worked well and in no time, we had checked in the bags, made our way through security and were eating breakfast at Pret a Manger. Terminal 5 is really a shopping precinct with planes visible through the windows. I drifted through the shops. It was quite surprising to see Boss, Burberry, Calvin Klein, Fortnum and Mason, Hanley's, Paul Smith, Ted Baker, Watches of Switzerland………. Amazing. The Western world in all its materialistic glory. There was nothing I wanted from any of them. There wasn't very much I could have afforded. I got some mints from W.H. Smith and prepared for the call to the Gate.

The luckiest break was that I'd somehow ended up with a seat near to the emergency exit meaning that I had more leg room. Perfect. We set off at 9.50am. The smoothest of flights to Nairobi. Long distance flights aren't something we should aspire to. The amount of carbon emitted on

I climbed Kilimanjaro - and learnt things.

my flight was enormous. I can't hide from that. The fact that I was trying to raise money for a sustainable travel charity called 'Ridewise' wasn't forgotten. What a contradiction. Having committed to make the journey I was determined to ensure it was a valuable experience, that was not just about having a holiday. Could my trip make the world a better place? I hoped so, though I confess to not being crystal clear as to how this might happen. The money raised for 'Ridewise' was a small part of it. There had to be something bigger. It was on the ascent itself I realised that by sharing 8 lessons others might benefit. I have just about persuaded myself that the lessons go some way towards offsetting my carbon footprint.

That said I happily watched 2 films as we soared above Europe and North Africa. The first, 'Aisha', was an intense story about a Nigerian girl who was trying to get asylum in Ireland. Food for thought. I then trivialised things by watching Julia Roberts and George Clooney in "Ticket to Paradise". I was feeling morally balanced as we landed in Nairobi. It was 9.00pm and it took us an hour to emerge from the bubble of security, passport control, visa checks and vaccination re-assurance. During that time, I struck up an interesting conversation with a chap called Darragh from Glasgow who had re-trained in his 30's to become an expert in wild animal welfare having previously worked in a tax office. He was on his way to a meeting with a colleague from Dar es Salaam in Tanzania with a view to finding a solution to a problem caused by lions who had become confident enough to move into a town in southern Kenya. Nobody wanted to shoot them, but the locals were, understandably, nervous. I'm always interested in hearing from people who change their lives by taking a radical decision that would terrify others (If you've made one then please get in touch). My new friend had certainly pivoted into a new world. I do hope the lion issue was sorted out.

I had been a bit surprised when the nurse at my GP practice had told me that I was too old to have a Yellow Fever vaccination. I wasn't particularly concerned about her reluctance to give me the injection because the risk of the disease affecting me seemed slim in the areas I planned to visit but when I heard the officials asking others for their Yellow Fever certificate, I can't pretend that I didn't flinch. Could I really be sent back to the UK at this early stage? Sure, enough I was asked if I had been vaccinated and when I told my inquisitor that I was over 60 he just nodded and waved me through. Being elderly does have its advantages it seems.

Ian had joined the wrong queue- don't you hate it when that happens?- and was 15 minutes after me in breaking free of the administration zone. He wasn't best pleased. It was the first sign of Ian in Victor Meldrew mode. There was a long running TV series called "One Foot in the Grave" in which a mature gentleman played by Richard Wilson gets angry and flustered day after day, hour after hour. I know I have my moments too. But Ian has a special talent. The fact that his Irish Passport hadn't brought the anticipated advantages seemed particularly galling.

Outside the airport it was hot and lively. Cab drivers were keen to persuade new arrivals that they were the best and most reasonable in the business. It was our first contact with the 'free for all' that is East African transport. We followed a friendly Arsenal supporter to his car and had soon arrived at the Crowne Plaza hotel. It was guarded by two uniformed security officers who raised the barrier when they were persuaded that we arrived in peace. The backpacks were cleared by the airport style security machine, and we entered a hotel that was just as we would have expected to find in London, Dublin, or Paris. Tiled floors, rubber plants and helpful staff. We had paid more for this stopping off point than anticipated but it was close to the airport and the beds seemed likely to be comfortable. There was also a bar that was still serving food so we both ordered pizza. I had a beer, Ian – only an occasional drinker- had cider and I had a picture taken with the Chelsea supporting waiter.

It was midnight when we returned to the room. Sharing a room with anyone other than Anne was going to be a new and potentially awkward experience. The first night passed without any snoring complaints and we were up at 7.00am ready to grab breakfast, remind each other to take our malaria tablet then take the hotel shuttle back to the airport and await the arrival of a bus that would take us to the Tanzanian border and, eventually, the town of Moshi at the foot of Kilimanjaro.

Into Africa

Ian had booked the bus online whilst still in the UK. It was due at 8.30am and by 9 there was no sign of it. There wasn't really an obvious place for it to stop. A few WhatsApp messages were exchanged in which the bus booking person apologised on behalf of the Nairobi traffic. It was sunny and warm. Who cared?

At 9.15 a bus appeared. It looked like it might be going to Tanzania though why it is hard to say. A young chap jumped off and waved. He shouted "Moshi" to us, and we showed him the ticket that confirmed we were ready to fill 2 of the remaining 3 seats on the 18-seater. He and his mate pulled back a tarpaulin that was covering the luggage rack and threw our packs on top of the bus. In 10 minutes, all was re-assembled and the bus pulled off into the remainder of the Nairobi rush hour. There was one more stop to be made with a young nun being collected from a lay by on what proved to be the edge of the city. The tiny woman took her place in front of us and had a semi-heated discussion with the conductor about payment. She certainly didn't get a free trip. Maybe that was what she was angling for, but my Swahili wasn't up to the challenge of de-cyphering. We moved on.

The bus rolled along a single carriage way with stalls alongside selling fruit, shoes, gaudy shirts, pots, pans, and scrawny chickens. The land initially looked agricultural but soon turned into a yellow wilderness with the odd family of skinny goats roaming around with a young lad seemingly instructed to keep an eye on them. As we drifted away from the city the pop music channel that had filled the air changed to silence. It was a welcome relief. I dozed, looked out of the window, and dozed some more. I resented the sleep because it seemed such a privilege to be in Africa and I wanted to savour the moments. The landscape was like nothing I had seen before. Eking a living out of what was on view must have been so, so difficult.

After three hours we stopped at a service station. It lacked the sophistication of Gloucester Services on the M5 but did a job. There were toilets, lots of African souvenirs for sale and a caravan selling drinks and snacks. I started to chat to the only other non-African on the bus. I must add that his race had nothing to do with this decision. I chose him merely because he was standing alone.

It turned out he was called Al and was from Dublin but had been working in the mines of Western Australia for the previous 2 years. He was taking a one month break to visit the pyramids of Egypt, take in a safari in South Africa and climb Kilimanjaro. It emerged in conversation that he was from Crumlin in the north of Dublin and on hearing that Ian was from the south of the city he said "Ha ! The enemy". No fights broke out. 6 other small buses came and went before we moved on towards Tanzania. And within an hour we were at the border.

It took 70 minutes to get into Tanzania from Kenya. Apparently, that was quite brisk. First of all, there was a security check with our unloaded packs being scanned. For what I'm not sure but the soldiers with guns and stern faces seemed very keen to study the readings that the machine offered. Passport and visa control involved photographs, fingerprint checks and rigorous analysis of documentation. The men - there were no women on the other side of the desks - were keen to show they were extremely serious about their jobs, but I did wonder if anyone was ever rejected. Again, the health certificate check identified my over 60ness and, therefore, ineligibility for the Yellow Fever vaccine.

As we waited in the queues, I was befriended by a burly man from Dar Es Salaam who was clearly keen to speak with people from England. He was larger than life both physically and in terms of personality. I didn't catch his name, but I did find out that he was a medical doctor who had studied in Nottingham, Bristol, and Dublin. His career seemed to involve telling others how to do their jobs. There were no stories about treatments he had been responsible for and quite a few about how negligent others had been. Each anecdote was followed by loud laughter. He was entertaining company. Ian became involved after an initial reluctance and our doctor named him the "Bishop of Dublin" to his obvious delight. The doctor's not Ian's. He then considered a name for me and, after toying with "King Charles" he eventually settled upon "The Captain from the Sound of Music". I quite liked that but resisted the temptation to break into a chorus of "Edelweiss". We shook hands and said our goodbyes. The doctor wished us well on Kilimanjaro and warned us to be careful because the altitude could be dangerous. This kept cropping up.

We jumped back onto the bus and awaited departure. Young women knocked on the window in the hope that we would buy souvenirs. None of us did. There was then a particularly loud hammering on the window. One that couldn't be ignored. The doctor's face smiled through the glass. He was holding a notebook.

"Please give me your email addresses my friends" he said. I wrote mine for him. So did the Bishop of Dublin though he later told me that he had put in an extra letter to avoid further contact. I am not sure what he was worried about, but you can't be too careful, I guess. The chances of the Doc of Dar es Salaam appearing in Quorn seemed, to me, miniscule but I suppose I might hear one day that he was in Nottingham asking if anyone knew where Captain Von Trapp lived.

One person left the bus at the border. There were lots of buses around and presumably it was a key transition point. The journey continued through physically inhospitable land. Dry, yellow, flat. There were no fields. Nobody seemed to be even attempting to live off the land. Over the next 2 hours we were stopped three times by charmless armed police officers who insisted on checking passports. They boarded and hopped off with only a brief word for the driver. Rumour had it that the checks usually required the driver to pay a charge to the police. It seemed believable. Later on in the trip we saw signs about how corruption should be reported and some that boasted "This is a corruption free zone". Perhaps the passport checks were the first signs of dishonesty being a disturbing issue.

As we approached the city of Arusha the land started to undulate, and the colour changed slowly to green. There were signs of farms as the land moved to a higher level. Settlements became more substantial. In the distance we could see mountains emerging from the plain. A vicar sitting behind me said that the biggest one visible wasn't Kilimanjaro, it was Mount Meru. Meru is, like Kilimanjaro, a dormant volcano. It hasn't erupted since 1910 and that was only a minor flutter. Mount Meru stands 4562m high and is said to be good preparation for an ascent of Kilimanjaro with climbs taking 3 days and having less risk of altitude sickness. Perhaps one day.

Arusha is a city of more than 2 million people. It's huge. If we had attempted to go in and out of the city by bus it would have taken up to 2 hours, so it was something of a relief to find ourselves on a ring road which by-passed the city. On another day it might have been fun to explore Arusha but after 6 hours on a small bus on a hot East African Friday the appeal was limited. There was a stop though and 5 people left the bus with another three joining us for the last leg to Moshi. Amongst them was a small woman of Asian heritage who lived in London. She was delighted to converse with us- well me mainly. Ian just listened. 'Suella'- as I named her- after the then Home Secretary of the UK Suella Braverman- was an advocate for stricter controls of immigration into the UK. She sounded and looked like Ms. Braverman. 'Suella' was of Indian descent but had been brought up in Arusha before heading to the UK for work 20 years earlier. She lived with her brother in North London but had recently been made redundant and had decided to take a break with her parents for a couple of months. Despite her less than liberal views she was stimulating company, and we spent an hour disagreeing civilly.

At 4.00pm 'Suella' pointed out the first appearance of a mist shrouded Kilimanjaro. She told us that she had once attempted to climb the mountain when in her 20s but had given up after 2 days. It had been too hard. She hoped to give it another go. And she was sure we would be fine. Well....

We passed Kilimanjaro International Airport – the place we probably should have flown into thereby avoiding the need for a Kenyan visa and an 8-hour bus ride. However, the bus journey had been quite an experience. Not one to be missed. And then suddenly it was over. The driver pulled off the main road into a hotel car park and there, behind the trees and next to a school, was the hotel that we were heading for. Ian and I were the only ones to be unloaded. We wished 'Suella' well for her relaxing break if not for her plan to deport refugees to Rwanda.

The journey had already provided opportunities to meet people. I think Ian and I had done pretty well. We had been friendly and interested. It's for others to decide if **we'd** been interesting! The Kilimanjaro experience re-enforced my appreciation of the importance of connecting. It is such an important skill.

Life lesson 3: Networker – nicely !

"Every friend starts out as a stranger"

Terri Nakamura

More to follow……

The team assembles.

As we descended from the bus we were immediately met by a small team of greeters. They were clearly well schooled in welcoming G Adventurers to the Stella Maris Hotel. "Welcome my brother" said the lady who was obviously the boss. Whilst one young man took our bags, a young woman offered a drink, and another guided us to the reception desk. They took our details and carried the backpacks to a room which had 2 four posters with drawn back mosquito nets and a balcony that faced the still shrouded mountain. There was a simple but adequate bathroom. It was feeling like Africa now. I remembered 'Out of Africa' with Meryl Streep and Robert Redford. It never occurred to me back in 1985 when it was released that one day I would go to East Africa. But then it hadn't really crossed my mind until July of 2022 either.

An hour after our arrival we heard a cab pull up. Ian's son Daniel and daughter-in-law Emma had arrived. They had flown from Entebbe in Uganda to Kilimanjaro International ready for the latest stage of their Round the World honeymoon. I warmed to them both immediately. Interesting and interested people who could both tell a story and listen to one. They were clearly going to be easy to work with over the next week or so.

Daniel (Dan) was keen to book a meal in Arusha and I was delighted to let him take the initiative. As he was organising the booking and ensuring a cab would take us there and back, I could hear a presentation being made to a group of G Adventurers who had just returned from their attempt to conquer the mountain. It emerged later that all but 2 of the 12 had completed the climb and amongst the successful were a 65-year-old American woman and her brother who was 2 years older. When we spoke to them later that night, they provided some re-assurance with regard to older people being able to reach the top but stressed the need to go very slowly and at your own pace.

"If others go more quickly you need to ignore them and stay in your own mental zone," said the brother.

And we were to be under no illusions. "It is really, really tough," said the sister. I also noticed that whilst there were 2 older people the rest of the group appeared to be under 40. But the 60 somethings made it. Good news. Maybe I was dealing with an appropriate challenge after all.

The taxi was due at 7.30pm so Ian and I followed a sign to the upstairs bar. Sitting alone awaiting her evening meal was a woman called Laura.

She was from Wicklow in Ireland and was travelling alone. Laura was in our group. Her sister had completed the Kilimanjaro challenge some years earlier and had told her about the starry nights, the interesting people, the camaraderie – and how very difficult it was to reach the top. The YouTube clips and articles that I'd read in early December were on the right lines. This wasn't going to be a cake walk but there was to be no backing out now.

As we chatted with Laura her pork chops arrived - and Kilimanjaro emerged from the clouds. It was spectacular. The sun was setting and reflected off the mountain. It was like every promotional photograph available on Google images. The challenge had shown itself and it was formidable. Within a couple of days, we would be invisible presences on its slopes. We would be immersed in slowly taking one step after another as we edged ever closer to the summit.

The meal was a relaxing experience. The restaurant had two covered areas where the diners ate, an outside bar and a kitchen area that seemed to be a hive of activity. It seemed that the customers were comfortably off locals. We appeared to be the only tourists. I ate pork with chips and had a couple of beers. A well-behaved dog sat looking at us clearly hoping that we might offer him a snack. Was Africa so different from England?

I slept reasonably well behind my mosquito nets. At breakfast I chatted with Laura from Wicklow. We agreed to battle it out for last place in the line as "slowly, slowly" seemed to be the key to success. My previous experience of meeting up with groups told me that it was helpful to know your companions well without overwhelming them with curiosity. Laura was happy to reveal that she was 31 and was an investigator for eBay. What a job. It hadn't occurred to me that such roles existed. Another hidden job. (Check my podcast series **" I DID YOU CAN"** for more)

Laura told me that she was going to take Diamox during the trip. I had acquired some Diamox tablets before I left England. It had been a late decision. Buying it from the internet without a medical examination didn't feel right. I guess it was another risk. Diamox is supposed to reduce the impact of altitude but also increases the urge to urinate. That isn't a side effect that a man in late middle age welcomes- how many times can you visit the toilet during the night? - but I decided to add it to my morning array of medical supplements. I took half a tablet every day. Did it make a difference? It's so hard to tell.

Laura had visited Moshi the previous day so turned down our suggestion that she join us as we paid it a visit on that lovely, hot Saturday morning. Armed with sunhats, Factor 50 sun block and fly repellent we set off for the town. It took 15 minutes to get there. Moshi is the capital of the Kilimanjaro region. It was originally set up by the German authorities (Tanzania was handed over to the British in 1919 after the First World War) as an important railway settlement dealing mainly in the transport of bananas. Since then, it has become the main base for attempts to climb Kilimanjaro and for safaris. In March the Kilimanjaro Marathon attracts people to Moshi from all over the world for what is now an iconic event.

Moshi is a sprawling place. Dan, Emma, Ian and myself drank teas and coffees in the cushioned and quite delightful 'Blossoms' coffee house. 'Suella' from the bus had recommended it. We could have been in the Cotswolds rather than a bustling African town populated by people who were never likely to sip a Flat White in the shade of a wicker roof with jazz playing reassuringly in the background. Moshi or Moreton in the Marsh?

We drove past Mweka College which runs courses in Animal Welfare management and the Mawenzi Regional Hospital which apparently is "grossly underfunded" and in 2010 was closed down for a period of time because inspectors judged it to be "dirty......lacking ventilation ....and dangerous." Some extra funding appears to have raised standards and it has now re-opened. Norway it seems has close links with the hospital and every year physiotherapy students spend a year working with those experiencing orthopaedic difficulties. It seemed likely that anyone facing problems on Kilimanjaro might well end up at the Mawenzi Hospital.

When we emerged from the soothing atmosphere of 'Blossoms' we faced a wall of heat as it was now approaching noon. In February the temperatures are consistently above 30 degrees in Moshi but then in the coolest months- usually June and July- it rarely dips beneath 25 degrees. The streets were alive with stalls selling fruit, shoes, shirts, pans, sewing machines and weighing scales. One part of the town had 8 men sitting at sewing machines making adjustments / repairing items that had been brought to them. We were the only obvious tourists to be roaming the streets and not surprisingly that attracted attention. Emma, as a blonde-haired woman, seemed to be particularly interesting. There was no unpleasantness. Just fascination. But that's easy enough for me to say as a sixty something white man.

We were back at the Stella Maris by 2.00pm. That gave us some time to relax and take stock before the team briefing that was timetabled for 6.00pm. I made a few notes, read a bit of my book (Jonathan Franzen's 'Purity' for the curious. A bit disappointing if I'm honest) and walked alongside the main road for a while. At one point a truck passed by with a jazz band sitting on the trailer. When they saw me, they waved excitedly and started to play. Such a colourful way to live. There were a few houses that hinted at wealth, but most were best described as shacks with corrugated iron roofs. As I returned to the hotel, I saw children streaming away from the area in brightly coloured clothes. I had heard singing as I ate breakfast and I later discovered that Saturday was a school day, though a shorter one and one that didn't require uniform. The Stella Maris hotel's profits went to support the school which had been set up largely to cater for orphans. There were 300 children at the school, most of whom lived with grandparents in the area. It is estimated that there are 1,300,000 orphaned children in Tanzania and that HIV has been the major cause of this. 'Blossoms' might have felt like Middle England, but it was clear that Tanzania differed in a thousand different ways.

At 4.00pm I was sitting under the sun canopy on the point of falling asleep when I heard a voice saying "Mister. The briefing sir". It turned out that the team briefing had been brought forward from 6.00pm to 4.00pm because everyone had now checked into the hotel. I roused myself and found the briefing room. When I entered there were 6 youthful faces sitting around a long table, plus Ian. Another 2 equally fresh-faced characters soon arrived. The group leader introduced himself as Kajeli. He was from the local area and spoke in an assertive/aggressive manner which immediately made me feel a little uptight. I didn't feel any better when he circulated a list which had our name, nationality, contact details and age detailed. I couldn't help but see that I was the eldest at 63 and, after Ian, the next oldest was Dan at 34. Whilst the reality was tricky to deal with the fact that everyone else knew so much from one sheet was a bit troubling. Was I that sensitive? Not really, but personal data is protected in the UK and here was a Canadian company playing fast and loose with it. There was no point getting excited and so what if I was more than 30 years older than the rest of the group?

The usual circuit of introductions took place. I already knew Ian from Dublin – though he'd lived in Leicestershire for nearly 40 years – Dan and Emma from England, but living in Germany, and Laura from Wicklow in Ireland. To that select band were now added Sophie and Laura from Melbourne in Australia and their friend Vicky, a Canadian who now also lived in Melbourne. Chad from Ohio in the USA and Iggy from Norway were travelling alone and completed the group. All seemed like pleasant people who were keen to push their frontiers. And so, it proved. But they were so young. And I was so old. There was no hiding from it. Later that week Laura from Melbourne said, "Hey Phil did I hear you say that your youngest daughter is 29?" " 'Fraid so" I replied. "Oh my God, "said Sophie. "That means that your youngest daughter is older than the three of us." It was true.

The briefing went on and on. I could see why it was necessary but much of it was beyond torturous. The majority of what was said had already been detailed in notes that had been available a month earlier. Kajeli was duty bound to tell us about equipment, the rental agreement, the expectation of punctuality, the route, food, altitude, sleeping arrangements, the porters - known as 'Dream Makers'- and the role of the group leader or CEO (Chief Expedition Officer). He explained that we had the option of using the long drop toilets or paying extra for a portable loo and tent. The long drop didn't seem a sensible option so there was agreement that we would pay $25 each for the alternative with one of the porters charged with ensuring it was emptied, cleaned, and carried from base to base.

Kajeli also led us through the chants that would be heard. If we heard someone shout "G" we were to respond with an enthusiastic "Adventures". That would be followed rapidly by a shout of "Adventures" and we would bellow "G". Straightforward enough. Similarly, if someone led with "Don't stop" the expected response would be "To the top".

The briefing lasted more than 2 hours. The will to live was steadily deserting me. It had been 4 years since I had been involved in long, boring meetings. I had lost the ability to feign interest. At the end we were introduced to Emmanuel who was to be our group leader. He seemed like an agreeable chap, and so it proved.

When the briefing ended, we ate together and chatted. I sat next to Iggy from Norway at the first meal. Iggy was in her mid-20's, the youngest of the group, and was a solo traveller. She was one of the fortunate ones who had a tent to herself. It was clear that Iggy had seen a lot of the world already having ventured to the Himalayas, South America, and several European countries. Her English was, of course, exceptional. Which young Scandinavian does not speak English as well as, if not better, than natives? Later she told me that she had not yet settled into a job or a relationship and was happy travelling- even if her mother wasn't quite so content with her lifestyle choice. I wasn't sure how she managed to fund her travels as she had recently had a temporary job at a nursery. It can't have been a big earner.

Dan seemed to know more about football than me. Rare. It was relaxing to compare thoughts about the English Championship with him supporting Sunderland and me having long ago committed myself to Wigan Athletic. The football chat was a relaxing escape from the intensity of Kilimanjaro speak and the comparing of travel CVs. I went to bed ready for the adventure to start properly on Sunday. "Don't stop to the top". Indeed.

The climb starts.

I sat in the foyer waiting for the departure. Saturday was to be my last night with a decent amount of sleep. I think I had slept on and off for 5 hours or so. My newly rented 4 season's sleeping bag and large black duffel bag were at my feet. The backpack had been placed into storage along with the items that wouldn't be required for the adventure. Ian and I were the only team members to have retired from full time employment. It struck me that I had probably spent more time thinking about the trip than most. That perhaps wasn't healthy. Whilst I was determined to do everything possible to get to the summit the thought had sometimes crossed my mind that I might not make it. How would I deal with that? To come so far, tell so many people what I was doing, raise money through sponsorship.... and then fail! My dentist, Mr. Shah, had a friend who had given up after 2 days. As failure entered my head, I immediately banished it. Positivity was all.

The squad followed Kajeli's punctuality orders to the second. By 9.00am we were on the bus heading to Moshi to acquire extra snacks, hire clothing, collect hiking poles, and make sure we had enough money from the cash machine to tip the support team. Tipping was a hot topic. There was general feeling amongst the group that rather than rely upon tips the porters and guides should really be paid a decent wage. It had been suggested by Kajeli that every participant should contribute $250 to the tip fund with extras for individuals who had helped in a special way. We had paid a lot for the expedition. How much would go to the team of local porters – or Dream Makers? It remained a troubling question, but I was re-assured to have heard that G Adventures treated their teams well.

The supermarket was more like a large corner shop, but I managed to acquire enough mints, sweets, and biscuits to see me through the week. I had also brought 3 bars of Kendal Mint Cake (a product to support fell walkers in the English Lake District) from home. So, what could possibly go wrong?

The equipment hire store was in the basement of a concrete office block on the edge of Moshi. We followed each other into a tightly packed cellar which was chockful with all the kit anyone could need for an ascent of the largest mountain in Africa. My enquiries had of course suggested that boots and down jackets were not available for hire. They were. Along with anything else you cared to imagine. I picked up an extra water bottle, a thick fleece, and some ski trousers as well as a pair of hiking poles. Ian didn't bother with the poles. More of that later.

As I sat on the bus with my younger colleagues and youthful support team, I did feel a little daunted. I could have been back in England reading 'The Observer' or walking the dog. And very pleasant both would have been. But life is short, and I never yearned to not be facing the challenge. In my opinion to feel truly alive you need to do things that challenge you whatever your age. That was the fourth lesson from Kilimanjaro that I will explore in section 2.

Life lesson 4: Challenge yourself to do great things

"You are never too old to set another goal or dream a new dream"

C.S. Lewis

More to follow......

To the Macheme Gate

It took the best part of an hour for us to complete the rentals. This was not surprising as some of the group had Kilimanjaro as just one piece of their adventure portfolio and needed to hire virtually all the kit required for the higher levels. The journey to the Macheme Gate from where we would start the climb took over an hour. It was past noon when we disembarked the bus. I'd estimate there were at least a dozen other buses depositing climbers into the car park. American and Australian accents mingled with French and Italian tones. I heard some English voices but not many. One bus delivered just Japanese people. The team had prepared lunch for us and presented it in a series of plastic boxes. It was the first experience of catering Kilimanjaro style, and the quality of the picnic was high.

By 1.30 pm we had eaten, visited the toilets, topped up our water bottles and had a photograph taken at the start of the Macheme route. It is perhaps worth saying a little about the routes to the top of Kilimanjaro.

The most popular route is called Marangu sometimes called the Coca Cola route. It's the most popular one probably because it is seen as the easiest. If any route can be called easy. The slopes are relatively gradual, and it has huts which tend to attract the less experienced travellers and that perhaps explains why only 35% of those taking this route actually make it to the summit.

The most expensive route is Lemosho. It is a newer route, and the extra cost is due to more time being spent on the lower slopes in order to assist acclimatization. This does seem to work with 90% of those who start finding their way to the top.

The Shira route seems a bit of a cheat. Participants are taken by vehicle through the rain forest of the lowest slopes meaning their first engagement with the mountain starts at 11,000 feet. Whilst that speeds up the process it also means that the lack of acclimatization reduces the chances of success and only 75% manage to get the peak.

Rongai approaches from the north. It's the only one that does and tends to come into its own in the rainy season because of its position in a rain shadow. The paths are gentler but the scenery less attractive. 80% of those using this route end up at the top.

And then there was our chosen route. Macheme, or the Whisky route. The name was given to it because it contrasted with the Marangu route. It's considered much tougher. Hence Marangu being dubbed Coca Cola and Macheme named Whisky. A drink for tough guys, I guess! Macheme is considered to be the most beautiful with a variety of landscapes, but it is difficult, steep, and usually selected by the more adventurous. How I ended up on it is anyone's guess. The Macheme route is 38 miles long and 85% of climbers make it to the top. That of course means that 15 out of every 100 don't do it. Would I be one of that select bunch? Hopefully not.

Sunday afternoon : Through the forest

At the Gate we waited for our duffel bags to be weighed. 15kg was the maximum allowed. Given that they would be carried on the heads of porters it seemed absolutely appropriate that this was checked rigorously. We had our day packs checked too. Water bottles, snacks and rain proofs were fine. Alcohol and illegal drugs were not. And then we signed the form to say we were entering the National Park. It was 2.00pm. We were ready to go.

The first section of our climb took us from the gate to the Macheme Camp. Moshi is 915m above sea level. We had left it behind that morning for the Macheme Gate which sits at 1634m, and we were heading for the

Camp at 2834m. It took us from 2.00pm to 7.00pm to cover the 10km and climb 1919m. The path was initially quite gentle but soon became more challenging. The whole stretch took place in dense rain forest. At one point two of the rarely seen Black and White Colobus Monkeys appeared high in the trees and hung around long enough to be photographed. At this early-stage shorts and T shirts were worn. It was perfect weather for a stroll in the woods.

I could hear conversation taking place between our "20-something" friends. It wasn't the sort of stuff that a "60-something" retired Principal with 3 grandchildren was going to engage in, but it was innocent enough and cheerful. There was an air of optimism and excitement as people got to know each other and absorbed their new environment. Porters passed by laden with the heavy gear. Other groups passed by occasionally. Always I was minded to keep the pace slow. "Pole Pole" was the Swahili warning. It was more difficult than anticipated and I must confess that Laura from Ireland was outclassing me in the slowness stakes. At one point she was told to speed up because for this stretch there was only one group leader and we had to stay close together. So much for "Pole Pole".

By the time we arrived at the Camp it was nearly dark. It had the feel of a French campsite in that there were lots of tents, plenty of excited people and lights coming on across the place. The toilets weren't like anything seen in Brittany, however. An early visit confirmed what we had been warned about. A wooden hut covered a hole in a timber floor. The smell was revolting. The long drop of the toilet was less long than it might have previously been as detritus crept closer to the surface. The team investment in a portable loo was a smart move.

It emerged that each team of porters raced to get the best sites on the campsites. Our tents had been erected by the team on very solid land. It can't have been easy to hammer the pegs in. So presumably they hadn't

I climbed Kilimanjaro - and learnt things.

won the race on this occasion. Each tent was named after a character from 'The Lion King'. We were allocated Pumba. The others were Timon, Nara, Sarafina and, of course, Simba. I'd heard of him. I took photographs of each label to show my 3-year-old grandson. No one else did that. I wonder why?

Inside the tent that was to be shared by two 6 feet plus gents were our duffel bags which contained sleeping bags, extra clothes, for use as the temperature dropped and the wind picked, up and a towel to help us dry ourselves after a very limited daily wash. Ian and I decided the duffel bags should be placed at the end of the mattresses near to our feet. This proved to be an error. Sleeping with legs bent was never going to be comfortable and after day 1 we used them as a dividing line between our two halves of the tent. There was a zip up entrance on each side. That design feature was helpful, especially in the middle of the night.

We had our evening meal at 8.00pm. It was impressive. Three courses. Soup to start with, a main course of pasta and tomato sauce and cake for dessert. Throughout the trip we all shook our heads at the way the catering team managed to create dishes that tasted good and also provided the nutrients needed to equip us to face the challenge confidently. We chatted for a while afterwards. Everyone seemed relaxed. The Aussie / Canadian trio were clearly good fun, but it was Laura from Ireland who got the best laugh of the night with her response to my announcement that I was going to bed followed by Ian saying he was too.

"Did anyone ever see Brokeback Mountain?" she asked with a deadpan expression. Great film but neither Ian nor I felt especially comfortable with the reference ...... to the delight of the rest of the team. For those who don't recall it was a 2006 movie about two cowboys, played by Heath Ledger and Jake Willenhall, who discovered love whilst camping out in the wilderness. Did that make it difficult for me to sleep? It didn't make the slightest difference. The chances of me getting much sleep were always slim. It was my biggest worry before I set off and it proved to be an appropriate one. I read. I made notes. I lay on my mattress until 2.00pm. Wide awake. I then put on my headphones to listen to podcasts. Maybe I slept, maybe I didn't. I would say 2 hours of not being conscious was the maximum that I experienced.

the mountains are calling...

Monday : A steep climb to Shira Camp

At 6.00am the porters tapped on the side of the tent to wake us and kindly provide a hot drink. I appreciated the cup of tea, but the reveille wasn't necessary. I was wide awake however it was time to leave the tent and prepare for the day. I was feeling weary but the thought of another day on the slopes was exciting rather than daunting and adrenalin meant the lack of sleep wasn't too troubling at this stage. I assured myself that I would sleep better for the rest of the trip. I wasn't a stranger to camping. I had regularly slept under canvas as a boy, had run a campsite in Spain in my 20's and been on a lot of camping holidays in Europe with the family. But I was younger then and my body's aversion to sleep had not kicked in. It had now. I was also aware that altitude can play games with people's sleep patterns.

Breakfast did what was required. Coffee, hot chocolate or tea, porridge, omelettes. An energy fix to push on to the next camp. The conversation was lively too in our green dining tent with the collapsible tables and chairs. We were ready for action by 7.30am. Monday was set to be a more demanding day across steeper terrain, but the sun was shining and the views over the East African plain already jaw dropping.

We walked all morning up a steep and rocky path. It was slow going because all the climbers and their support teams seemed to have set off around the same time. Understandably we were expected to step to one side when the heavily laden porters passed by. Despite the packages on their heads, they seemed to bounce along, often chatting, singing, or listening to music. "Jambo" they would shout as they passed by. It would be rude not to respond so I would shout "Jambo" back. By the end of the day, I had learned that it was the Swahili word for "Hi". I also picked up that "Mambo" was a more informal response but meant the same. So, I started to use that too. Virtually bi-lingual.

The rainforest was left behind as we moved into a rockier and more open terrain. It was described in the brochure as "alpine". That seemed like a fair description. Every hour or so we would take a break. The instruction was that we would drink at least 3 litres of water every day in order to help keep altitude sickness at bay. Snacks were also important to keep blood sugar levels high. The brief stops also allowed everyone to search for an appropriate toilet. This was easier for the males it has to be said. The women in the group were happy enough to find a spot in the wooded areas to relieve themselves but it became increasingly difficult as the landscape changed. Boulders became more and more precious as the search for some privacy intensified.

One of the beauties of the hike was the opportunity it offered to find out more about our travelling companions. I spent some time talking to Chad from the USA. He was a single guy in his early 30's who had hiked all over the USA. He had reached the highest point of all but 4 states and had also climbed to the Everest Base Camp and to Machu Picchu in Peru. It was clear that Chad knew a lot about hiking in mountainous areas. Ian and I joked that he had become our role model even though he was 30 years younger than us. He had the best kit, a great hiking CV and offered tips to help us walk more effectively. Deep breathing was one that stuck with me. The use of poles to take the strain was another. But Ian chose to ignore that one!

We arrived at the Shira Camp at 1.30pm. It had been a long but lovely morning. Machame Camp had been 2834m above sea level and we were now at 3840m. We had ascended over 1000 m in 6km. My knee was hurting a little but otherwise I felt in fine form, though pleased to have a few hours to relax and recover- perhaps even sleep a little.

The camp was set up at Shira and we had lunch before some free time. At around 4 we were offered the chance to visit some caves with one of the guides called Marwa. He explained that until the year 2000 the porters had few rights. They would carry the bags and be fed but it was up to them to find somewhere to sleep and often the caves were the answer. It had been freezing cold, the snow could blow in and, not surprisingly, some porters died. Others must have had their lives shortened quite significantly. After 2000 the companies running the trip- mainly local entrepreneurs in the early days- were legally obliged to provide shelter, food, and care for the support teams.

Much of the porter's story still remains uncomfortable I'm afraid, though it did appear, I'm pleased to note, that G Adventures had a reputation for best practice. There is a massive over availability of young men willing to work on the slopes. Little wonder therefore that the cost of a team of porters for a typical ascent is often less than the food bill for the customers. I was shocked to find out that some still die on Kilimanjaro. It is usually exposure combined with exhaustion and poor clothing that leads to their demise. And some of the company's seem to think "Plenty more where they came from". No longer do they sleep in caves. Now they usually sleep in overcrowded tents with maybe 10 of their colleagues. It was encouraging to hear that the Kilimanjaro Porters Assistance Group has made a significant difference to the life chances of the teams. This involves lending mountain clothing to porters free of charge, advocating for fair wages and ethical treatment by all companies climbing Kilimanjaro, encouraging climbers to select a climbing company with responsible treatment practices towards their crew and providing educational opportunities to the mountain staff.

After our trip to the cave and the somewhat harrowing stories the porters and guides entertained us with the mountain lurking in the background. The team gave us a few Kilimanjaro classics with the biggest hit being Jambo Bwana.

Hello, hello sir.

How are you ?

Very well ?

Guests- you are very welcome.

Walk slowly. Slowly.

No trouble.

You'll get there safe.

No trouble.

Drink plenty of water.

No trouble.

And so on. It works better in Swahili I feel.

There were others. 'Malaika' and 'Kilimanjaro' were two that grabbed the audience and even encouraged a few dance moves from the audience but not, I hasten to add, from myself and Ian. We stood by and clapped enthusiastically. Dan did a pretty impressive snake like dance. It had a name, but I don't recall it and I haven't got the enthusiasm to carry out any research to discover it.

All the team then introduced themselves and told us their role. There were people who searched for fresh water, another who rather heroically looked after the toilet, some who cooked and acted as waiters, tent erectors, guides of course and Emmanuel the leader. If they were unhappy, they didn't look it. We were then asked to introduce ourselves by saying our names and where we came from. A lovely event. The mountain looked on admiringly.

It was becoming colder. We were now at 3840m so not a surprise. The shorts hadn't lasted long. From now on hiking trousers and a fleece would be needed. The oximeter tests for oxygen and heart rate were carried out. Again, I wasn't comfortable with personal data being shared with the whole group but didn't feel strongly enough to rock the boat. My figures were 86 and 67. Yesterday they had been 90 for oxygen and 67 for heart rate. Everyone else's seemed pretty similar. No stand outs yet so we all lived to fight another day. We had been told that if the oxygen figure dipped below 80 and heart rate above 80 then further consideration to our continued participation would need to be given.

Just to emphasise the importance of health checks I need to mention the helicopter landing pads that had been created at key parts of the route. On 3 occasions I heard a helicopter on its way to assist a no doubt panic-stricken climber who was facing serious difficulties. Kilimanjaro does kill people. The Tanzanian authorities and the travel companies are reluctant to share mortality figures but in 2003 a researcher called Markus Hauser reported that around 7 people a year died on the mountain and that was when far fewer climbers were on its slopes. There is also little information about people who end up with long term disabilities due to the effects of high altitude. Nobody expects to be struck down, but the helicopter is always coming for someone. Gloomy I know.

Mealtime was already exposing the personalities of different people. Ian has no embarrassment gene. He was involved in banter with the Australian / Canadian women. They could give as good as they got, and they were helped by Dan who was always quick to tell his dad when he'd overstepped a mark. It was always innocent enough stuff and created lots of laughs. I remember the trouble he got into when he described Laura, Sophie, and Vicky as "typical Australian girls "and then struggled to clarify what this meant. I'm not sure I helped by putting some words to him that might help him throw light on what he was trying to say. "Promiscuous "I tried. "How dare you?" laughed Laura as I found myself sinking with Ian. I didn't get so involved again. The atmosphere in the dining tent was great as was the food. I didn't make a note of every meal, but my scribbles tell me that on Monday we were served with vegetable soup, rice with chicken and a sponge cake. Pretty good for 10,000 feet above sea level. By 9.00pm I was in my sleeping bag preparing for sleep.

Life lesson 5: Be a team player.

"Alone we can do so little, together we can do so much".

Helen Keller

More to follow

Ian was already away. As I lay on the slopes of Kilimanjaro awaiting sleep, I reflected on how the team of 10 visitors was quickly bonding and how the support team was operating so effectively. The power of teams.

Tuesday: Up to Barranca Camp

The use of podcasts might or might not have meant that I slept a little better. I had set up Dr Rangan Chatterjee series "Feel Better, Live More" to help me through the previous night when sleep had proved no less attainable. That must have been around midnight. Usually, I get to sleep and wake up to go to the loo followed by a frustrating inability to not return to sleep. This time I wasn't even dozing off in the first place. At midnight I put on my headphones and let Dr C converse with a wide range of experts on topics ranging from "Avoiding burnout", "How to heal chronic pain" to "How kindness can improve your happiness". I dipped in and out of sleep. I don't recall dreaming anything, but I must have slept a little. However, when the porters knocked on the side of the tent to deliver cups of tea, I was far from revived.

We left behind Shira Camp and headed up the slope across a barren alpine landscape. At the start of the day's hike, it was clear. Kilimanjaro was glistening in the distance. As we climbed mist swirled, it got colder and windier. Rain seemed possible. We reached Lava Tower (4630m above sea level) for 1.00pm and stopped for lunch. Each company had set up a temporary dining room. The wind was hammering the sides of our tent, thunder rumbled in the distance. The plan was that we would stay at this high level to get used to the higher altitude before descending to the Barranca Camp which was 500m lower. As the rain started to fall a few of us were getting a little anxious about walking down the slope on a stormy afternoon. Lightning strikes? Was it a possibility? By the time we had eaten, the weather had calmed a little and we were able to travel to the Barranca Camp with a minimum of fuss. I chatted to Vicky who lived in Melbourne but had spent much of her life in Canada. She now had an Australian boyfriend and had followed him back to his homeland from North America. He was aware that she was following him- and supportive- she assured me. Vicky was training to become a counsellor alongside her office job and was hoping to be professionally active in the next year. She was far from the most serious member of the group. Every evening, she would have self-deprecating tales to tell. My favourite was the one about her being in a romantic embrace with a 6-feet 8-inch basketball player in a Florida night club. As she was only a shade above 5 feet tall there was quite a gap between her feet and the floor, and she told how her little legs were kicking the air when her friend arrived to say she was going home. I've tried a form of words to get the comedy across. I think I've failed miserably to do it justice. Contact Vicky's agent. I'm sure she'll be on tour at all the big venues soon.

The Barranca Camp was at the foot of the 300m Barranca Wall. It looked above us with a menace that could lead a sensible person to ask, "Is there a way through?". I was, however, aware that crampons and ice picks would not be required because there was a path- admittedly a steep one - that minimised most risks. The Wall cropped up a few times in conversation over dinner – another high-quality pasta dish - but I didn't detect anyone being especially spooked by it. Emma admitted to feeling a little weary. Hardly a surprise given the miles she had covered since her wedding the previous summer. I had noticed that she had gone from initial bubbliness when we dined in Moshi just 4 evenings earlier to seeming quiet and a little withdrawn. She told me she too had been having problems getting to sleep. She had brought with her a natural remedy that helped a bit she thought, but we both knew that rest mattered and neither of us were getting enough sleep, it seemed.

Wednesday: Over the Wall to Base Camp

The night was very cold. I slept with thermal underwear and a fleece but still shivered a lot. Barely any sleep came my way. Again, I tried using my phone to soothe me to sleep. My "Moody Mix" playlist might have sent me over the edge to sleep for short periods, but it was another tough night and for once I didn't feel better after breakfast. The Frankfurter sausages just didn't do it for me. I had one but left it half eaten. Altitude can play games with your appetite, and we were at 3950m above sea level, but I suspected the nature of the sausage offering was a bigger villain than the height of the land.

Emmanuel had consulted us about the start time and the consensus was that we should aim to begin the climb of the Barranca Wall at 6.45am rather 7.30. Why hang around watching others set off? So, by quarter to seven we were ascending the Wall. It was intimidating but only rarely was the heart anywhere near the mouth. I later saw a picture of Sophie apparently clinging to a sheer face. Friends have gasped. Oddly it never felt troubling. But it did go on for 2 hours and I did need my wits about me. However, the lack of sleep meant my wits were not always that accessible and I found myself stumbling on a couple of occasions. No one seemed to notice.

Sophie was the quieter of the three Melbourne based members of the group. On the first evening we had been talking about films that we loved and when I said "Notting Hill", the classic mid 90's movie starring Hugh Grant and Julia Roberts she said, "My mum likes that too." And that summed up the generation gap!

I liked Sophie. She told me about the logistics role that she had. It sounded very responsible. I enjoyed hearing about her trip to Ireland with her mother some years earlier. I know Ireland quite well but the places that I would have expected them to visit had been avoided as her mum preferred the small towns to Dublin, Galway, Cork, Derry, and Belfast. They must have had a uniquely Irish experience. Australians do like to see the world.

I climbed Kilimanjaro - and learnt things.

My conversation with Sophie's best friend Laura was illuminating. Laura was a confident young woman. She also had travelled widely as Australians do and had considered living in England, but her partner was an electrician and suspected that his trade would not earn the same respect in the UK as it did in Australia. This has long been an important topic for me. So many people complain about the lack of electricians, plumbers, and joiners, yet the education system rarely encourages a young person to pursue a route that could lead them to a trade and rarely do middle class professionals seem to respond positively to their son or daughter wanting to become a trades person. It's crazy. And the UK pays a price. I was grateful to Laura for raising the subject – and raising my blood pressure. It was fortunate the health check didn't take place at 11.30am. I would have been doomed.

After the Wall we trekked across a bleak, windswept plain, had another cooked lunch/ late breakfast, minus the Frankfurters, in a tent and finally arrived at Barafu Camp around 3.30pm. Base Camp. Kilimanjaro loomed large above it. We had covered 8km and ascended 650m, but it felt like more. The group had become divided into two as we crossed the plain and Ian had become oddly annoyed. Was the altitude getting to him? We had heard often enough that it attacked in different ways.

Our early dinner was followed by a serious briefing from Emmanuel during which he told us what to expect and how to prepare. The expectations were as follows (I think):-

1. Be ready to leave the camp site at midnight.

2. Be in the right mind set. The Summit Day involves a very steep and long climb.

3. Wear a headtorch and make sure fresh batteries have been inserted.

4. Wear warm clothes: 2 pairs of socks, 2 pairs of gloves, thermal underwear, waterproofs, wind proofs. I got the message.

5. Take snacks and make sure they are accessible.

6. Keep your water deep in your pack. It could easily freeze.

7. Accept help if it is offered by one of the team.

And finally: 8. Get some sleep between 6 and 11.00pm. Oh yeah. That seemed likely.

So, to bed. It was barely dark. I lay there. I tried reading, listening to music, thinking. Nothing worked. At 11.00pm we were 'awoken' by the team with the customary cup of tea. Perhaps those awaiting execution had similar feelings as to what awaited them. I made sure I was dressed for what was to come. All instructions were followed. I had been lying for hours in my sleeping bag with thick socks, thermal underwear a shirt and a fleece. Now I added the thick fleece I had hired, my recently purchased down jacket, waterproof coat, and ski trousers. The woolly hat, face covering, two pairs of gloves and boots completed my attire. As I set off in the line at 12.05am on that Thursday morning I felt overdressed, but it was Kilimanjaro. Who knew what awaited?

Thursday: to the Summit and Back

Thursday was a very long day. I remember starting with a feeling of exhaustion already running through my system. I was running on empty, but I had confidence in my ability to focus on adversity and achieve the goal. I had run 2 marathons some years earlier and, yes, the last few miles were very hard. The Ashby De la Zouch 20-mile race was also horribly uncomfortable with a torrential rain shower soaking us at the start. My failure to go at a sensible pace to begin with and a lack of snacks meant that I actually ended up walking for a mile or two, but I finished. I got there. I had cycled quite long distances and some of the steep hills had made me grimace and ask myself why I was doing it. But I did it. Always. Obviously, Kilimanjaro would be the same. I never doubted that I would get to the summit. Well, not when we set off at least.

I was in my own world. The sky was clear, the air was cold, there was no wind. I looked at the stars. Breathtaking. Some members of our group were talking, but I was silent. After an hour we had the first stop, Emmanuel stressed that it needed to be brief because if we stayed for more than 5 minutes the cold would start to hurt us.

Ahead were hundreds of fellow climbers with headtorches lighting their way. At 2.15 we stopped again at one of the many bends on the rocky route. I was feeling reasonably well. Tired but not doubting that success awaited. A bite of a biscuit. Some Kendal Mint Cake. Let's go again. Step after step. Pole, pole. Slowly, slowly.

At 2.30 our support team burst into a chant of "G. " " Adventures" " Adventures G". A chorus of the Kilimanjaro song. Experience had told them that it was reaching the point when spirits needed to be lifted. Oddly enough the singing coincided with a dip in my wellbeing. I sensed that my body was not as eager to move as it had been. I looked forward to the next stop ......but it was 50 minutes away. Something must have been odd about the way I was moving because one of the support team asked if I was feeling OK and walked alongside me for a little while. Some of the guides had completed 200 or more ascents of the mountain and experience told them the signs of difficulty. As I was over 60, I'm sure they had a careful eye on me anyway. The next stop didn't last long enough. 5 minutes felt like 30 seconds. And I was too hot. I suspected I was overdressed but there had been such an emphasis placed on keeping warm in potentially dangerously cold weather that I had made sure I was protected. I took off a pair of gloves, a linen scarf and my waterproof jacket and marched ponderously on.

Every step was feeling more difficult to take now. The gradient hadn't changed. I looked forward and saw the line of climbers disappear. Did that mean we were at the top? No. It was a mirage. The line had just rounded a bend. The zig zag route went on and on. I felt seriously tired. My legs were dealing with the challenge, but I just wanted to sit down on a rock and fall asleep for an hour. Obviously, that would be disastrous. One of the most experienced guides, Marwa, sat alongside me and asked if I needed help. I admitted that I was finding it tough, and he said "Everyone does. Did you think it would be easy?" Without waiting for a response, he said, "Come on".

I walked alongside Marwa for 20 minutes then took a break, then another 15 minutes. Walking for an hour without a break was totally unthinkable. My head felt scrambled. By 5.30am if I had been offered a zip wire back to base camp I would have hopped on immediately.

"I don't think I can do this Marwa" I said.

"Well, why did you come to Africa?" he asked.

"To climb Kilimanjaro." I replied.

"Then climb it." Marwa instructed. So off we went.

I climbed Kilimanjaro - and learnt things.

At 6.00am, the sun was starting to brighten the sky. I noted the sunrise and have since admired photographs but frankly it was just a note in the margin. Marwa took my bag and put it over his shoulder. That eased things a touch. I had no idea or interest in where the rest of the group was. It was all about me, Marwa, and the mountain.

We were edging closer to the end of the steepest part of the climb. Stellar Point and the end of the steepest part of the slope awaited. The sun had now risen. Headtorches were switched off. As I got close to the top, I could make out Dan. He was leading the rest of the group in a chorus of "Wigan, Wigan". Hearing my football team's name chanted made me smile. Dan later told me that he didn't know any Wigan songs. I told him that "I'm a Believer" by The Monkees was the big one. Now that would have really lifted my spirits.

I arrived at Stellar Point. I'm told I was 10 minutes after the others. I cared not. I was just glad to be there. As the rest of the group trudged wearily off to the Summit, I genuinely felt my climb was over even though the path to the Summit was less dramatic and probably less than an hour away. I just wanted to sleep.

"Marwa. I'm done. I can't go on." I spoke.

"Ok. It's 30 minutes of work or 30 years of regret." said Marwa. He had probably said it a hundred times to different shattered, English-speaking climbers. It worked. The thought of not getting to the very top would be hard to deal with. My brain recognised that. Similarly, he touched a nerve when I said Stellar Point was fine by me.

"Are you a silver medal or a gold medal sort of person?" he asked me. There was only one answer.

I told a friend of mine about the choice of medals and he said "I'd have said I'm a bronze medal sort of person. Can we go down now please?" I have seen photographs of me with the team at Stellar Point. I looked old and weary.

10 minutes from the Summit I passed the other 9 team members making their way down. They had wanted to wait for me so we could have a photograph together, but Emmanuel had insisted that they didn't wait long at the top. The dangers of altitude were real.

Arriving at the summit was wonderful. Such a relief. The hardest work was over, I thought. I had a photo taken alone, and then with Marwa and Emmanuel. In the photographs I look at the difference in my face between Stellar Point and the Summit. It is like years had fallen from me. But then the descent began. In truth it was much easier. Yes- it was a treacherous scree slope. Yes, I vomited on the way down – I'm told that's common. Yes, Ian the man who didn't need poles did take a tumble and probably cracked a rib – the guides insisted he use poles for the rest of the descent. Yes- it took 4 hours to cover the 8 kilometres back to the tent at Base Camp. And I was still so very weary. But compared to the climb it was a doddle.

It was wonderful to see the Base Camp, but I was disappointed to find that we still had to walk more than a kilometre to reach our tents. The wind was blowing dust across the site and cloud was now covering the mountain. I opened the entrance to the tent and collapsed onto my sleeping bag. Bliss. Even as a I type I can feel the pleasure of feeling it was over. In truth it **wasn't** over but there was to be no more discomfort that approached the levels of that morning in Tanzania. After an hour we were beckoned for a meal. I stayed where I was. Emmanuel came to check that I was well. It is so unlike me to turn down food but the pleasure of lying down could not cease quite so quickly.

By half past three we were told that it was time to move on. As we put on boots and jackets, the tents were already being dismantled by the porters and soon they would be overtaking us with bags, chairs, tents,

I climbed Kilimanjaro - and learnt things.

and toilets on their heads. The walk was largely flat and mainly dry. But it was cold, windy, and dusty. There was little to see but it didn't matter. Endurance was all. At one point we passed what looked like an elongated supermarket trolley with thick tyres. Emmanuel explained that this was how injured or sick people were moved from the mountain to the hospital if they could not afford helicopter support. They would be carried down the steeper slopes and then transferred to the stretcher/ trollies before meeting up with an ambulance closer to the exit from the National Park.

By 6.00pm, we had reached the Millenium Camp, the last camp of the adventure. I was ready to eat and even slept a little that night. In my notes I'd written "It's been a ludicrous day. So painful". At the risk of sounding a little like a speaker on Radio 4's "Thought for the Day" I can't resist saying:

"And sometimes life's like that but you just have to keep going and usually the discomfort ends."

> **Life lesson 6: Expect discomfort -and battle through it**
>
> "Growth and comfort cannot co-exist"
>
> Ginni Rometty
>
> More to follow......

Friday: Job done.

More sleep. Not much but some. I'd been up in the middle of the night to visit the toilet and noticed one of the porters acting as a security guard. It seemed that they did hourly shifts because in the past thieves cut into tents sprayed the sleeping climbers with a gas that knocked them out and taken their belongings.

The tea arrived a little later today. It was 7.30am. A lie in. We were breakfasted and ready to walk by 8.30am.

But first there was more entertainment. The porter team assembled. The mountain was in the background. Conquered. And for one last time the gang sang and danced. This time it was celebratory. No need for encouragement. They had also been given their tips. This was made up of a $250 contribution from each member of our group. It was collected by Vicky and handed over to Jackson one of the guides who would ensure fair distribution. There had continued to be discussion amongst us as to how much the porters and guides were paid. Was the tip their payment? Jackson assured me they were paid properly, and the tip was just a bonus but I for one was unsure about this. Further research suggests they are paid as little as $6 per day in some cases. I believed that G Adventures was one of the better employers, but the nature of the role means that contracts are rare, the work sporadic (with none during the wet season) and with the supply of young people willing to do the work far exceeding the demand. Inevitably this kept wages low and working conditions worse than they should have been.

We were thanked by the people that had worked so hard for us over the last week and then an eerie silence. As the elder statesman I felt duty bound to step up to fill it. Frankly, not a hardship. I'd really missed addressing school assemblies.

"On behalf of our group" I said "Thank you so much. It has been a privilege to be with you for the last week. We have been amazed by the amount of work you have done- carrying, supporting, cooking, guiding, finding water, singing, dancing- just amazing. And smiles have almost always been on your faces. Thanks so much. This has been the experience of a lifetime. I would particularly like to thank Marwa who persuaded me that it was possible to get to the top of Kilimanjaro when I was starting to doubt myself. I know other members of our group have got similar thoughts about different members of your team. Thank you so much."

Dan then moved forward and said "You have been incredible. Obviously without you we would not have made it to the top, but you've worked alongside us, and I hope that you have felt like partners. Thank you. Thank you."

There was applause. One last song and then we disbanded. I sought out Marwa to give him my last $50 and promised that I would send him a Wigan Athletic shirt." I will wear it at the summit and send you a photograph " he assured me. Given the poor form that my team had been in I suspect he might fold the shirt up after the one viewing and keep it in a locked cupboard.

We had a long 14km walk to the end of the hike to the Marweka Gate from the Millennium Camp and were now in shorts and T shirts again as we left behind the less hospitable upper slopes. The path was downhill, often steep. It started to rain as we worked our way through the forest meaning the rocks were slippery. A broken wrist or sprained ankle at this stage would be a little disappointing so we took care. Even Ian was using poles by now.

I stayed near the front of the group and chatted a little with Jackson. I was interested to hear him speak French to two women who asked for directions. He told me that he had been learning to speak the language to accompany his fluent English because he hoped to become a safari guide. The more strings to his bow the better he thought. He said he spoke a little German too but had not taken lessons in it.

"Why is it better to be a safari guide?" I asked him.

"This is so hard. Rich people don't do this. Their children become lawyers and businesspeople" he told me. "I am 30 now and don't want to keep climbing the mountain. I am happier now I am a guide and not a porter, but it is still very difficult. On the safari you just drive a jeep and point at lions and giraffes. Much easier."

He was smiling as he spoke, but he surely had a point. Obviously, the guides and porters were used to the climb and the carrying. They had often been doing it for 20 years. But it could never be easy and the strain upon the human body must be enormous. I wished him well on his desire to progress to the safari world.

It was clear that we were coming to the end because a track with tyre marks had emerged from what was a rock-strewn pathway. As we walked, we heard a vehicle coming up the track.

"Stand back, it's an ambulance," said Jackson. And sure enough, a blue and white Land Rover style ambulance appeared. Obviously, it was on the way to assist someone who had come to Africa to complete a challenge and was going to end up in hospital. I suppose if there was zero risk and it was a straightforward thing to do, fewer people would sign up. But it made me think.

I walked alongside Laura from Wicklow as we got closer to the end of our trek. She told me that she had travelled alone because her partner hadn't been keen to come along but her sister had completed the climb a few years earlier and had found it exhilarating. She just had to do it and fortunately eBay, her employers, allowed her to take a sabbatical every five years. Laura was going on to complete a safari when we finished. It turned out that the other Laura, Sophie, and Vicky from Melbourne were also going on the same safari along with Chad and his 70-year-old father who was on his way from Portland. I hoped one day to find out how Chad's dad had found his interaction with the 'Melbourne gals'.

I climbed Kilimanjaro - and learnt things.

I had told Dan that I would be at the front of the group with our leader and compared it to a cyclist at the Tour de France who had made a breakaway. He reminded me that the rest of the peloton almost always reeled in those who tried to get away. I was not to be caught though and arrived at the gate before the others. I don't think anyone either noticed or cared!

We had photographs taken at the exit sign which congratulated us on completing our goal. As we waited for the next move, I was approached by a man who I naively thought was the bus driver. He asked if I would have my dusty boots cleaned. He took me to a hose pipe and within a minute they were spruced up. He clearly expected payment. I offered him 10000 Tanzanian shillings and just as he was about to take it one of our guides appeared to make it clear that the note was to cover Sophie and Vicky's boot cleaning too. He accepted with a gloomy face. Later I realised that I had paid him £3.50. Not a bank-breaker.

We waited in the modern office block at the Maweka Gate for exit documentation to be signed off. Such clean toilets. And then we boarded the bus. There were 6 other buses with similarly weary travellers looking out of the windows as they left the Kilimanjaro National Park. After 20 minutes we pulled up at an Arts centre which had a restaurant and souvenir shops. The meal was good. Chicken, chips, and vegetables. The beer was refreshing. Sadly, I knocked mine over in my excitement to consume it. Alongside us a couple of African guys played guitar and sang. It was relaxed and, much as the food in the tent had been appreciated, it was better to not be under canvas.

The shop had the usual stuff. T shirts, fridge magnets, postcards, cuddly toys, hats, and key rings. All had a Kilimanjaro theme. I selected a blue T shirt that I was sure I would treasure until it became just another running shirt. In truth the most important souvenir would be my notes, my memories and the photographs that supported them. We had agreed to share the best photos using an app that Iggy had found.

As the bus rolled into Moshi, I could see Emmanuel talking to two of the guides. They seemed to be reviewing what they had learned from the week. What had gone well? What could be better? There was no doubt that Emmanuel was a good leader and that he had made a difference. They always do.

> ## Life lesson 7: Consider leadership
>
> " If your actions inspire people to dream more, learn more and become more, you are a leader "
>
> John Quincy Jones
>
> More to follow......

Friday evening: The team breaks up.

On the 50-minute drive back into Moshi we passed stalls selling more souvenirs, fruit, and meat. The bustle of town life was increasingly evident. And then we arrived at the Stella Maris hotel. Back where we first met. The lovely staff were there to congratulate us and offer celebratory drinks. They certainly knew how to put on a welcome. After being allocated to our rooms -rooms with proper beds, showers, air con – we washed and then came downstairs for the review meeting with Kajeli. Surely it wouldn't take 2 hours. Luckily it didn't.

As he worked around the room asking for our views of the trip, I became aware how uneasy he was. Our first meeting had suggested he was a bit arrogant and condescending but in truth, as so often is the case with people, he was lacking a bit of confidence. This meant that he was a little defensive when even a mild criticism was made. I made a big deal of the impressive teamwork that we had witnessed and how he should be proud of the people that worked for him. I also named Marwa as an inspirational figure. Others tapped the table in agreement, I hope the compliments were noted. I also wrote them down for the online review so G Adventures could hardly complain that they hadn't been given any feedback. It was good that they asked for it.

Then as the sun was dipping, we sat under the outside canopy and awaited the award of the certificates. Inevitably, Emmanuel said they would give out our awards in age order. I was thrilled!

"First of all. Age 63 and a half years is Philip Crompton."

The crowd cheered. I raised Marwa's arm in the air and thanked him again. And I returned to my seat feeling relieved it was all over.

"Second. Ian Marron. Age 59 years."

That was the grandads dealt with.

And then it was the 20 somethings.

There were hugs and thanks to Emmanuel, Marwa, Jackson and Kajeli. Obviously, we were just another group of westerners that they had helped but they seemed sincerely cheered by our happiness. There had been a group the previous week and a new one would arrive the next day. As we set off on the next stage of our travels they prepared to say hello, carry bags, set up tents, sing songs, answer the same questions they had answered the week before and be pleasant as they did it. I bow to them.

The meal was great. A team had emerged. A shared goal. Shared adversity. Shared success. We had so much in common now despite age, nationality, and gender differences. Chad– and his dad, 2 Lauras, Vicky and Sophie were leaving the next day to spot lions, giraffes, and hippos. Iggy was heading independently to Zanzibar before flying to South Africa. I was going to have a few days relaxing in Zanzibar with Ian, Dan, and Emma before making my way back to Nottingham via Mombasa, a train, Nairobi and London Heathrow. That's another story.

Over the next week I pondered how I could make best use of the Kilimanjaro experience to help myself and others grow and fulfil their potential. That's how Section 2 emerged.

Time to leave the Crowne Plaza in Nairobi

Loading up in Arusha

The first view of the Kilimanjaro.

Back, from left to right: Ian, Phil, Laura from Melbourne, Vicky, Iggy, Dan, Emma.

And the front: Laura from Wexford, Chad, and Sophie

The camp. Night 1

The dreaded long drop toilet- looking innocent.

Barranca Wall- looking scarier than I recall.

The team always enjoyed a photo opp. Who built the bridge?

Ant and Dec ? Mortimer and Whitehouse ?

Or Crompton and Marron -the intrepid mountaineers?

Stellar Point. The steep bit's done. "30 minutes more hard work or 30 years of regret?" -as the man said.

With my friends Marwa and Emmanuel At the Summit. They couldn't have done it without me !

A pleasure to be part of this team for a week. Energy, commitment, laughs, support, and amazingly good food.

We climbed Kilimanjaro.

Even the 63-year-old veteran!

Yep. I did it.

And if "I, DID YOU CAN" -as the podcast said.

But I did get a little help from Marwa - and Miley.

"It's The Climb".

Section 2

8 lessons from Kilimanjaro

There was a lot of time to think on the slopes of Kilimanjaro. Occasionally, the thinking took place as I walked, listened, and observed but a lot of it happened as I lay awake at night. I found it so hard to sleep. That was frustrating, but the upside is that I used the time to reflect.

I thought about the influences on the way our lives go and how they were brought home to me on Kilimanjaro. The thinking has been pulled together under 8 headings. If I had understood each piece of learning when I was younger who knows what might have been unleashed! But we all live our own lives and respond to the circumstances we find ourselves either in or emerging from. I'm more than happy about the way my life has turned out. I've been fortunate. But the 8 lessons from Kilimanjaro just might enhance the life experience of others. There may be people in their teens, twenties or thirties who are keen to get a little direction. And I'm sure there are more experienced people who are still prepared to adapt their lives. Never stop learning should perhaps be the 9th lesson.

It's important to be clear about one thing at this early stage. A satisfying life does not mean you have to be famous or rich. A life well lived can, of course, be low profile, completed without either great wealth or travel. However, it is worth considering a few people who have found their pleasures in significantly different ways and attracted some attention. How on earth does it happen? Perhaps by considering these characters who did extra-ordinary things we might start to reflect upon our own potential.

Sir Edmund Hillary and Tensing Norgay were the first humans to reach the summit of Mount Everest. Ellen MacArthur sailed around the world on her own. Marie Curie was the first woman to win the Nobel Prize. It was for her work on spontaneous radiation. She won it again 8 years later for her work on radioactivity. In 1926 Gertrude Ederle became the first woman to swim across the English Channel. In 1954 Roger Bannister became the first person to run a mile in less than 4 minutes. In 1928 Amelia Earhart became the first person to fly over the Atlantic and Pacific oceans.

Such remarkable achievements. And all done by human beings. Just like us they were born, relied on adults for a while, learned to do things like eat, walk, and talk and then they did amazing things. When they were babies, they didn't wear a wrist band that said, "Future record-breaking sailor "or "Soon to be Nobel Prize winner". They weren't born to achieve extraordinary things. Something happened to them at some stage of their lives to put them on track to the record books. There will have been lots of hard work and no doubt a little good fortune but none of their success was pre-ordained.

How did Amelia Earhart set herself the challenge of flying across oceans? It was unthinkable in the 1920's.

What possessed Roger Bannister to think he could run a mile in such a fast time? Very few people thought it was possible when his quest began.

Marie Curie was remarkable in being a groundbreaking scientist – and a woman. In the early part of the 20th Century, it was unthinkable that a female could make such amazing breakthroughs and then be recognised for her work. What changed her from being like most other people born in 1867 into becoming one of the most famous scientists in the world?

I pose these questions because I find it fascinating how some people fulfil their potential whilst others don't appear to. I have often thought about this subject and have come to a few conclusions: -

1. Some people are born with a remarkable gift. Mozart was writing musical pieces at the age of 4 for goodness' sake. Hardly anyone falls into this category.

2. Some people are born to parents who have a passion for something that is passed on to their children. It might be sport, music, art, science, or a technical skill. The child is so immersed in it from an early stage that a higher-than-average level of achievement is almost inevitable. The England cricketer Stuart Broad is the son of a professional cricketer. I think we can safely assume that he was surrounded by the sport from a very young age. His family spoke 'fluent cricket', had a wealth of contacts and no doubt provided many practice opportunities for the young Stuart.

3. Some people are encouraged to try a variety of things and are backed by enthusiastic parents. If they show talent, then parents provide the support required to help them make the most of their ability. The mother, father or carer might or might not have an interest in the selected area, but they encourage regardless. Tennis player Emma Raducanu won the US Open in 2021 at the age of 19. Her parents were academics. They gave her the chance to play tennis when she was just 5 years old but also supported her interest in basketball, golf, and skiing. Tennis seemed the thing Emma excelled at so that's where the support settled.

4. Some people discover a talent or interest at an early age and move forward because of their own personal commitment. They plan, set goals, train hard, practice, listen to others and emerge from the crowd. Gary Barlow was inspired by the work of Elton John and was keen to buy a keyboard after watching Depeche Mode on TV. He then entered competitions, found an agent, and toured the clubs of England supporting other performers before eventually emerging as a founder member of the famous boy band "Take That".

5. Some people do not realise they are good at something until their abilities are flagged up to them by another person. They have a belief that what they can do is not remarkable and that surely everyone can do it but as their confidence grows so does their skill/expertise and consequently they get closer to fulfilling their potential. I know a lot of people who are in this category. I put myself there.

6. Some people drift through life thinking they aren't very good at anything. These people look at others in either awe – "wow, they are amazing" or cynicism "s/he is just lucky". Occasionally they wonder if they could do more, but that glimmer of light is soon put out because they don't have the confidence or determination to do what is required to develop their interest. I've sometimes found myself in this category.

7. Some people discover an interest, and they show talent. The talent starts to be developed. They look as if they will move to the next level but then they realise just how much effort is needed to keep progressing. It's just too much. There are so many distractions and too little time. "I can't be bothered" is an oft used phrase by such characters. I've found myself in this category too sometimes.

8. Some people have no talent whatsoever. There are very few in this category.

I climbed Kilimanjaro - and learnt things.

My background

I was brought up in a quiet village called Garswood in the northwest of England. My dad was a telephone engineer, my mum had many jobs. Factory worker, cleaner, chip shop assistant and eventually she ran the stores at a Home Office radio depot. I had a younger brother who went on to work in the communications business. We had a dog called Beauty and went on caravan holidays in Great Britain. I supported Wigan Athletic, occasionally went to watch Lancashire play cricket and went to a pantomime every year. We weren't rich but we were far from poor compared to others in our village. I knew very few people who worked in offices. Socialising with teachers, police officers or businesspeople rarely happened. I was happy in my early childhood. When I went to Grammar School and had to mix with people who **seemed** cleverer than me, I found life more difficult. "Seemed" is emphasised because so many of us appear to feel like this. Others seem more talented, seem more confident, seem more likely to succeed.

What did life hold for me? Who knew? The conversation never really took place. I just drifted through my early life. Years later I read some lines in a book called "The Joy of Winning" by Michael Beer.

"Dolphins use the waves. They can't decide how big the waves will be, when they will arrive or where they will break, but they take each wave and decide: this one we will dive under, this one we will swim through, this one is good for surfing. They decide.

The bottle can make no decisions. The waves throw it around as they like. It is completely at the mercy of every ebb and flow until it is finally thrown out on the beach, rejected by the sea as something of no account or importance."

It is fair to say that Hillary, MacArthur, Earhart, Bannister, Curie, and Ederle at some stage became dolphins. Perhaps they always were.

I was a bottle that became **a bit** of a dolphin !

Acting upon the 8 Kilimanjaro Lessons just might create more dolphins.

I climbed Kilimanjaro - and learnt things.

Life lesson 1: Know yourself.

" A genius in a wrong position could look like a fool "

Idowu Koyenikan.

One of the wonders of the world is that everyone is different. How exciting is that? Every time I go to a sports event, a concert, a school, a hospital, or a hotel, I see people who have something in common for a period of time. They might even look and sound a bit alike. But they are so very different. The Kilimanjaro team united around a simple fact. We were all excited by the prospect of climbing the highest mountain in Africa. But we were all different in so many ways.

It's helpful to know what sort of person you are and what you can do to maximise your potential. Unless you know yourself, you will probably end up in a life that does not really suit you. I was briefly a trainee accountant. I had no interest and was probably seen as a bit of a fool. It quickly became apparent that I should explore another road. And so, I applied to train as a teacher. Thank goodness for that. I will not pretend that I was a 'genius headteacher' but I think I was competent, and I certainly enjoyed the life. I knew myself better as I got older. As we look at our lives, we need to consider what experiences will really suit us. Is it appropriate that you climb Kilimanjaro or are there other ways to help you make the most of your talents? Let's try to capture the essence of you.

Answer these questions. Don't think too deeply. It's best if you write down the answers.

1. How tall are you?

2. What colour are your eyes?

3. What is your favourite colour?

4. What would you love to have for dinner tonight?

5. What is your favourite drink?

6. What is the best film you have ever seen?

7. Where would you like to go for your next holiday?

8. What is your favourite piece of music?

Seven questions. The chances of anyone matching all your answers are small.

Here are my answers:

1. 184 cms   2. Blue (once described as dishwater grey!) 3. Yellow (sunshine !) 4. Lasagne (but with a shout out to chips and steak and kidney pudding) 5. Flat white coffee (or pint of Guinness) 6. Notting Hill (Got to love Hugh Grant surely?) 7. South Africa (or Germany) 8. " The Boys Are Back in Town" by Thin Lizzy (but as I get older various Joni Mitchell songs seem to be closing the gap)

I know I could ask 100 people tomorrow and there is only the tiniest of chances that anyone would give the same answers. And we've obviously only scratched the surface. Once we go into personality traits, appearance, past experiences, star signs and upbringing the gaps widen all the time. Well, perhaps star signs aren't that important. Though some may be interested that I'm a Gemini…. split personality type (all 1/12th of the world it seems)

If we are all so different it follows that what is right for you is not necessarily right for someone else. I thought about this on the climb up Kilimanjaro. All those people who had decided this was the right thing for them to do at that time. Some struggling. A few coasting. And most people in the world thinking that putting yourself in such a position was crazy. Why bother? There are lots of challenges that I would never consider; learning to speak Russian, to play the violin or to ride a Suzuki 650 just for starters.

The route you choose in life will inevitably have to be at least a little different from someone else if you are to become the person you are capable of being. And this goes for any age. You might be 14, 24 or 74. You remain different to your neighbours, colleagues, friends, family, and partners. Those differences can cause tension, but they can be liberating.

What sort of personality do you have?

There are various psychometric tests that are said to help you understand yourself better. The best known is the Myers-Briggs analysis. This was developed by a mother and daughter team in the first half of the twentieth century and involves asking participants a series of questions which lead to them being classified in one of 16 different personality categories. The answers indicate where you are on a spectrum in the following areas:

From Extraversion to Introversion

From Sensing to Intuition

From Thinking to Feeling

From Judging to Perceiving

The mother, Katherine, was intrigued by the way her husband seemed to see the world in a different way to her, so she started to consider the reasons for this. By 1945 the work she continued with her daughter Isabel was starting to be embraced by many larger companies in the USA. To this day it is used to help teams understand each other better. The theory is that, if you have people working or living in close proximity, they may annoy each other. If they were to understand each other a bit better than the friction might diminish, resulting in greater productivity.

I used Myers Briggs with senior leadership teams. It is an interesting tool. I emerge as what was classified as an ENFJ type : **The Teacher-** was the label it was given. A bit disappointing really. I was hoping for **The Commander** or **The Visionary** or one of the other exciting titles that were attached to the profiles.

ENFJs are *"idealist organizers, driven to implement their vision of what is best for humanity. They often act as catalysts for human growth because of their ability to see potential in other people and their charisma in persuading others to their ideas"* according to the M-B key. And that's fine. I guess that's how I saw myself.

I once had to work closely with an INTJ :**The Mastermind.** Apparently INTJs are *"analytical problem-solvers, eager to improve systems and processes with their innovative ideas. They have a talent for seeing possibilities for improvement, whether at work, at home, or in themselves."*

We were hardly Myers Briggs twins, more like polar opposites. Perhaps it was best illustrated through a diagram which related flowers to Myers Briggs personality types. I was in the Rose group: *"Thrives in warmth and brightness, companiable"* said the note, whilst my colleague was closer to Aloe Vera: *"Unique and rare properties, doesn't need attention"*. It worked very well for a while, but it involved a lot of compromise. It was a relationship that didn't end well. It could be argued that once the information is shared the participants are able to see their situation more clearly and all should be better. Sometimes people see their analysis and see no reason for compromise. They assume others will bend around them. That's awkward and needs to be carefully managed.

Isabel Myers Briggs herself said :

"When people differ, a knowledge of type lessens friction and eases strain. In addition, it reveals the value of differences. No one has to be good at everything."

HR departments have worshipped at the shrine of Myers Briggs for many years. There is now a lot of scepticism about its validity, but people are different and if Myers Briggs allows us to ponder our differences and adapt as required then the world might be a better place.

I made a comeback as a conference attender recently. The event explored strategies to improve the wellbeing of staff and I was delighted to be pointed in the direction of the VA Institute of Character. They have a survey which helps to identify your top 5 characteristics. After answering 90 questions it seems that my strengths are : Gratitude, Fairness, Curiosity, Social Intelligence and Humour. I'll settle for that. Especially as this analysis was free of charge. Check it out at : https://www.viacharacter.org/

None of us had any inclination to carry out in depth explorations of each other's characters as we trudged up Mount Kilimanjaro but even a superficial study of the team would have certainly identified different dominant personality traits. Would we have a long-term future as a high functioning team? Hard to tell, but we worked together well for that week with a purpose.

Does age make a difference?

Do we change as we go through life. Below are 21 questions that I conjured up. I answer as a man in his mid-60's living in rural Nottinghamshire.

What talents do you have ? I know a lot about football and politics. I'm good at mowing the lawn and cooking risotto. And omelettes.

What personality traits do you have? I am curious about the lives of other people. Meaning I like to chat, I guess.

What interests do you have? Reading- especially books by William Boyd, sport- especially football, cricket and cycling, politics, travel, and my family- obviously!

What do you feel passionate about? People who cheat- in a negative sense of course, the need for a more equal society and sustainable transport – and the fate of Wigan Athletic.

What would you like to change? The culture of the UK to one that's like Denmark

What would you like to achieve? I wanted to become a headteacher and lead a school to OFSTED " Outstanding". I did that and now think formal achievement is overrated. I'd now like to be seen as a kind person by friends and family.

What have you done well? Led schools. Been a good dad-I hope.

What do other people think others like about you? Cheerful- most of the time- and interested in others.

What do you think other people might not like about you? Lack of interest in material things. I don't much like cars. Nor cushions.

What's your biggest success so far? 3 great daughters. And I did the parkrun in 23.40 last month.

How was that achieved? Making them a priority. And training !

What is your biggest disappointment? Not spending more time preparing the world for " In Search of My Alumni" (the book that I wrote in 2019)

What caused that? Too keen to get a message out there about the way education continued to fail too many young people.

How might it have been avoided? Working with someone else. Asking more people to read it beforehand. Getting some early reviews for the cover.

What makes you laugh? Comedy that highlights how ludicrous politics is nowadays- and Father Ted.

What makes you cry? Stories about people overcoming huge obstacles.

What makes you get up in the morning? Milo the dog needs a walk.

What makes you want to stay in bed? A day without a structure.

What keeps you awake at night? A sense of not making the best use of my time.

What would you like people to say about you in 10 years' time? That I created some things that helped people fulfil their potential.

What do you think about these questions? I wish someone had asked me them when I was 14.

As we get older, we retain certain traits. They just don't go away. But experience leads to certain changes in the way we see ourselves and the world. Here are the answers to the same question that I **might** have given when I was 14- if anybody had bothered to ask: -

What talents do you have? Good defender at football, decent at sprinting- and the long jump, OK at geography and French.

What personality traits do you have? Helpful.

What interests do you have? Football, cricket, the Olympic Games.

What do you feel passionate about? Wigan Athletic and Lancashire Cricket team.

What would you like to change? Wigan get into the Football League.

What would you like to achieve? Do well in my O levels.

What have you done well? Played for school football team, ran, and jumped for the athletics team, got 10 /10 for a picture of Henry the Eighth that I drew when I was 12.

What do other people think others like about you? I listen to them and laugh at their jokes.

What do you think other people might not like about you? I'm a bit boring and shy.

What's your biggest success so far? An amazing goal line clearance for school team at Worsley Wardley.

How was that achieved? Right place at the right time.

What is your biggest disappointment? Feeling silly when I was asked to say a French word in the first year. It was "La règle".

What caused that? I had never said a French word before.

How might it have been avoided? French might have been started at primary school I suppose but not much I could do about that.

What makes you laugh ? Mike Yarwood (an impersonator on TV).

What makes you cry? The thought that everyone I know will die one day.

What makes you get up in the morning? Fear of being told I'm lazy.

What makes you want to stay in bed? Tiredness.

What keeps you awake at night? Nothing really.

What would you like people to say about you in 10 years' time? I don't know. No idea.

What do you think of these questions? It's the first time I've been asked stuff like this. It's making me think about what I might do with my life.

Now this all might seem trivial but it's combining to build something bigger. It's only when we have really given lots of thought to our lives that we can begin to think about what we want and where our priorities should be. At what stage should committing to climb Mount Kilimanjaro become a priority? Early in life and you can persuade yourself that you can do other interesting things- and there is plenty of time to do them. Later in life and you can feel that you are making the best of yourself- with fewer years to play with. How aware of yourself and your circumstances are you?

Awareness is what is going on around you. Self-awareness is knowing what you are experiencing. And how you respond to different situations. I respond differently now than I did 50 years ago. Of course, I do.

A button is pressed, and we see ourselves differently.

Sometimes you don't really know yourself until there is a moment of tension or crisis. When I was 21, Peter, a chap I worked with when I had my ill-fated stint as a trainee accountant, pointed me towards a quote from "Tender is the Night" by F. Scott Fitzgerald as he was explaining how my life might have been too easy and that I was not yet the person I would become :-

"And Lucky Dick can't be one of those clever men; he must be less intact, even faintly destroyed. If life won't do it for him, it's not a substitute to get a disease, or a broken heart, or an inferiority complex, though it'd be nice to build out some broken side till it was better than the original structure."

Peter was a very clever chap. I guess that what he was saying was that at some stage I would need to emerge from my comfort zone and deal with life at a different level. As I look back on my life, I can see that each challenging time I have experienced has helped me to see the world in a different way and my confidence has usually grown as I have realised that I can handle most things.

Different people: different choices

I am a big believer in not judging the life choices of different people. Each person will make decisions and, assuming they know themselves, that will be the right and proper decision for them.

Consider these different choices:

1. To stay in one place for the whole of your life or to move to another town, city, or country.
2. To go to university or straight into work at 18 – or 16.
3. To have children or not have children.
4. To buy a house or rent a house – or stay with your parents.
5. To live with a partner or to live alone.

6. To buy a car or find alternative ways of travelling.

Each decision influences the sort of person you become. There is no right answer. Maybe you have made the decisions and there's no turning back now. Maybe you are at an early stage of life and are considering one or more of the questions I've listed. Since I discovered the American poet Robert Frost's poem "The Road Not Taken" I've gained a deeper understanding of decision making. Just read it and see what you make of his thinking.

Two roads diverged in a yellow wood,
And sorry I could not travel both
And be one traveller, long I stood
And looked down one as far as I could
To where it bent in the undergrowth.

Then took the other, as just as fair,
And having perhaps the better claim,
Because it was grassy and wanted wear;
Though as for that the passing there
Had worn them really about the same,

And both that morning equally lay
In leaves no step had trodden black.
Oh, I kept the first for another day!
Yet knowing how way leads on to way,
I doubted if I should ever come back.

I shall be telling this with a sigh
Somewhere ages and ages hence:
Two roads diverged in a wood, and I—

Philip Crompton

I took the one less travelled by,
And that has made all the difference.

Frost, in my opinion, is saying that we all have decisions to make. Just make the call and live with it. There is no point dwelling upon it afterwards. Sometimes you might take a path that others find less appealing. It doesn't mean it is the wrong one. Linda Ronstadt sang that we all *"travel to the sound of a different drum"*. You make one life choice and I make another.

We all have life choices to make and inevitably each decision makes a difference. Who influences the decision making? Is it just you? Your parents? Your friends? Your partner? Your employers? Or do you avoid decisions and just let life happen? Sometimes the decision you make will lead you away from comfort. Others will be baffled and tell you that you are wrong. I am not saying you shouldn't listen to people who have followed the overgrown path and stumbled upon the traps that await but the decision must, in the end, be yours.

For what it is worth these are my answers to the questions I posed:-

1. To stay in one place for the whole of your life or to move to another town, city, or country?

I was born near Wigan. Lived there until I was 18, went to university in Hull and have worked in the East Midlands of England since I was 22. Time again? I would have gone to live in London at 22 and then gone abroad. Massive regrets? No. Just an itch.

2. To go to university or straight into work at 18 – or 16 ?

I went to Hull University. My school assumed I was on that path. I never challenged it. Regrets? None. I can however see why some people are tempted by the route that takes them to work as soon as possible.

3. To have children or not have children?

We were married at 27 and had our first child at 29. Regrets? None. But I know others who either delayed having had children, had them earlier – or not had children at all. There doesn't seem to be a correct way.

4. To buy a house or rent a house – or stay with your parents?

We bought a house at 27 and have owned / had a mortgage on 4 properties since then. We also rented between 2 moves. A house is somewhere you live. I was as happy renting as owning. In fact, I liked the reduced responsibility – less DIY. Regrets? Financially, owning has probably worked out better.

5. To live with a partner or to live alone?

I'm not great on my own. Others are. Living with someone else has been a winner for me. Not sure Anne would say the same!

6. To buy a car or find alternative ways of travelling?

If I lived in a big city, I would use public transport all the time. But I don't. So, I have a car and cycle or walk when it is practical.

I understand I haven't gone along very many overgrown paths. Rarely has anyone said "You are doing what? You must be crazy." Perhaps the leafy path would have led to greater happiness and prosperity. Who knows? Not much point dwelling on it. Just "think it through and do it" would be my advice.

And perhaps ponder the advice of the social influencer Mandy Hale:

"Growth is painful, change is painful. But nothing is as painful as staying somewhere you don't belong".

When you know yourself well you can set the right challenges and move forward. It might involve climbing Kilimanjaro. Or it might not.

If you would like to find out more about knowing yourself, check out my interview with Paul Harris on "I DID YOU CAN". He always knew what he wanted to do, and nothing was going to stop him. *Paul is a choreographer. He is best known for his work with the Harry Potter franchise especially for the wand fight in "Harry Potter and the Order of the Phoenix" but he has organised dance and movement on stage, TV, and film across the world. I met him when I was 11 but hadn't spoken to him for 40 years when we finally caught up on a Zoom call. It was no surprise to find out how his life had gone. From the age of 9 he had been a competitive ballroom dancer and continued to compete well into his 20's. Paul knew that his future would embrace the world of performance. He was sure at 11 and was sure at 19 when I lost touch with him. Such self-awareness is rare.*

Being a ballroom dancer cannot have been easy when you were brought up between Wigan and St. Helens in the Northwest of England. He was the only dancer that I met during my school days, and he attracted some comments that might be described as bullying but Paul says he never cared what others thought because he was on a journey to another world. Paul himself says the fact that he kept goal for the school football team and ran for the local Athletics club meant that the arrows aimed at him were deflected somewhat. It is important to note that there was no background of performance in Paul's family. It seems his grandad used to recite Lancashire poetry in pubs around St. Helens but beyond that, nothing.

After leaving school Paul lived in London, did a few clerical jobs to ensure he was able to afford to dance and then became a highly successful, professional dancer winning national and international titles before deciding that he would re-train as an actor. Success on stage and on TV followed but a chance meeting led to him being asked to choreograph the 1998 film "The Titchbourne Claimant" and a new career emerged.

Paul's work is also his hobby. He clearly loves what he does even though every assignment involves him working with experts who have the highest of standards. He thrives under the pressure. It doesn't feel like pressure because he is doing what he loves. There was never a likelihood that he would have a more conventional career. He knew himself well from the youngest of ages and the life that he had experienced as a boy was one that he was determined to immerse himself in. And it has worked.

Scan for the full interview with Paul.

My Kilimanjaro tips about knowing yourself are:

- Spend time getting to know yourself. Try things out. Play sports, read books, watch films, listen to podcasts, visit places, meet people, engage in work experience. You will like some things more than others. That's how it should be.

- Accept that everyone is different and what is right for your friend might not be right for you. If everyone liked the same things the world would be a dull place. Decide for yourself. Be a dolphin that uses the waves not a bottle that is bullied by them.

- **You will be expected to work with people who have different motivations to you. That can be tricky. Some people find satisfaction in different ways. The better you know yourself the better your decisions are likely to be. You will be more able to work with / around people if you feel at ease with the decisions you have made.**

Life lesson 2: Prepare well.

"Prepare to go. Before anything else preparation is the key to success"

Alexander Graham Bell

The day after the arrival at the summit of Kilimanjaro I asked myself if I could have prepared better. Could those difficult few hours between 4.00am and 8.00am have been made easier if I had spent more time preparing myself physically and mentally for the experience? Over the preceding months I had run regularly if gently, walked Milo the spaniel up hills- small ones, reached the top of mini-volcanoes in the Canary Islands and done 20 squats every day. I had watched 'You Tube' clips about the Kilimanjaro experience and spoken to people who had engaged with the challenge so I knew where and when the pain would come. I had taken Diamox and had all the necessary injections. But I could have done more.

I could have travelled to Switzerland and trekked at higher levels, climbed Mount Snowdon during the night and lost 5 kgs in weight. I could have checked what the temperature was likely to be during the summit attempt and adapted my clothing appropriately. I thought I had prepared well but I missed things and that was foolish, and nearly costly. It struck me that there's a lesson for life related to the importance of preparing.

Those who excel at interior decorating stress the importance of preparing the space that you intend to transform. Move out as many pieces of furniture as possible, cover the floor and any remaining larger items with polythene sheeting, sand down wooden surfaces, wipe clean walls and ceilings. Blimey it's tedious. Can't we just switch on the radio and start painting? Evidence would suggest that the most skilled decorators are blessed with patience and are able to ensure that before the first brushstroke is applied hours have been spent making sure all is ready for the perfect transformation. A less rigorous approach will lead to disappointment.

Similarly, a teacher who just turns up at a lesson with no knowledge of the ability of the class they are about to spend an hour with and assuming that their dazzling subject knowledge and startling personality will be enough to guarantee a stunning lesson will, almost inevitably, fall flat on their face.

Whilst on the slopes of Mount Kilimanjaro I thought about some of the great pioneers. People who over the years had stuck in my mind. I do not mean to suggest that my adventure was in any way comparable to what they achieved. In many ways we were part of a marketing machine that created the opportunity for us to do something memorable. The people I thought of broke new ground. They did things that made the world gulp. Did they just do these things? Or did they prepare? The answer is obvious.

Amelia's story

Amelia Earhart was a Canadian woman who grew up watching the Canadian Air Force pilots practice outside Toronto. Her appetite for this new type of transport was whetted. She went on her first flight in 1920 and by 1923 had acquired her pilot's license. Amelia was determined to maximise her impact upon the world. In 1928 she was a passenger on a seaplane that crossed the Atlantic from Newfoundland to Wales. This was part of Amelia's preparation for the challenge that would make her famous.

In 1932 Amelia Earhart flew solo across the Atlantic from Newfoundland to the north of Ireland (she had been aiming for Paris). It took 14 hours

56 minutes. She was the first woman to achieve this feat. It didn't just happen. She prepared herself in terms of knowledge, skills, and experience. If she had just arrived at an airfield and asked to borrow a plane so that she could fly to Great Britain I think we know what would have happened. Preparation was all. As Amelia herself said *"Preparation is rightly two-thirds of any venture."*

Roger's Story

In 1954 Roger Bannister was a medical student in Oxford when he became the first person to run a mile in less than 4 minutes. When Bannister crossed the line it was news all around the world. So many athletes had tried to get below 4 minutes. It had reached the point that it was considered impossible for a human being to run so quickly for so long. Once that psychological barrier had gone, others followed. Bannister's record lasted for only 46 days and the current mile record (it's rarely run these days) is 3 minutes 43 seconds.

Bannister always said that he had "prepared on a diet of pilchards, stew and a feeble training regime of 45 minutes a day". He even liked to have a drink of beer. His preparation worked though. In many ways the major battle was a mental one and he had tuned his mind perfectly for that challenge in 1954. It is also important to note that the new world record holder was training to be a doctor and had to squeeze his preparation into a very busy schedule. Others built upon his achievement by adapting their diet and training methods and went even quicker.

Ellen's Story

I love the story of Ellen MacArthur, the young woman from inland Derbyshire who prepared perfectly to sail around the world. In fact, not just sail around it but to become the fastest person to ever do it without company. When Ellen was a small girl, she read a series of books called "Swallows and Amazons" by Arthur Ransome. I read them too. They were based in the Lake District and told stories about a group of children who sailed dinghies on Lake Windermere. She was hooked by the sailing bug and saved her dinner money so that she could afford a dinghy of her own. She visited her aunt's home in Lincolnshire so that she could have access to the sea, taught at a sailing school near Hull and eventually was skilled enough to sail around Britain on her own. She was 19 at the time. 8 years later she had further developed her talent in order to traverse the globe in just 71 days. The fact that sticks in my mind was that she couldn't sleep for more than 20 minutes at a time for the whole of the journey. And there was me complaining about my lack of sleep over a 5-day period.

Like Amelia Earhart 70 years earlier, Ellen had prepared over a long period of time. In his book " Outliers" Malcom Gladwell popularised the idea that if someone practiced for 10,000 hours there is a much greater chance of excellence. That's a lot of time. One way or another Ellen MacArthur put that time in and, as a result, she was prepared.

Marie's Story

The great scientist Marie Curie grew up in Poland and, when her father lost all their money, had to end her formal education. She became a teacher and then a governess. Later she moved to Paris where she earned a degree in Maths and Physics. She married Pierre Curie and together they carried out important research which led them to a meeting with a well-known scientist called Henri Becqeurel. In 1905 the three of them were awarded the Nobel Prize for Physics for their work on radioactivity. In 1911 Marie became the first woman to achieve 2 Nobel Prizes. The second one was for Chemistry. None of this just happened. She experienced hardship, bereavement, and disappointment, but kept going. All the experiences and all her research were preparation for the challenges she embraced.

Gertrude's Story

Once I start to think about pioneers, those who go first, I become excited. I could write forever on the subject. I will end with Gertrude Ederle who in 1926, became the first woman to swim the English Channel. I have often taken a ferry from Dover to Calais. I have viewed those waters, and they are uninviting. Gertrude was an American who had always liked swimming. At the age of 16, she held 29 national and world amateur swimming records. In 1924, she competed at the Olympic Games but had to face the disappointment of not getting a medal and, in 1925, she failed in her attempt to swim the English Channel. It wasn't all straightforward for Gertrude. However, in 1926 she returned to Europe and became the first woman to swim the Channel. And her time of 14 hours 34 minutes was almost 2 hours faster than any man had swum it. She returned to her home in New York and received a 'ticker tape' welcome as she was transported through Manhattan. Her years of preparation had paid off.

A simple preparation guide.

Having committed myself to the importance of preparation it would be remiss of me not to offer advice as to how this should be done. Whether the task/challenge faced is short, medium, or long term, it's always wise to take a big piece of paper, write the challenge in the centre and then surround it with all the things you imagine need to be done in order to successfully achieve the goal. It can be anything- organising a party, a long-distance bike ride, the decoration of a room, the purchase of a house, winning the Nobel Prize for Chemistry...... dozens of things probably need to be done. Enjoy the "brain dump" as I believe it's now called. I'm uneasy with that term so I'll bravely return to "brainstorm". It sounds better to me, and I hope no one is offended. Go to town with it. Miss nothing. Throw yourself into it. Fill the sheet.

Then try to create some sort of order. What needs to be done first, second, third and so on. Just add a number. There is no wrong or right. And then leave it for a day. Let the water settle after stirring it. Tomorrow it will be still and clear.

When you return you might have come up with more points or have decided that some don't need to be done after all. And what were you thinking when you suggested that was the 5th thing you need to do? It's clearly less important. Everything seems obvious now.

And then write the list out from point 1 to point 51. Have a look. Does it work? It might need a tweak or two. When you are happy write down a date that you would expect to have done that particular action.

And make sure that your overall completion date is in big, bold, colourful capitals alongside the challenge itself.

Then keep it handy and start ticking things off.

This just might be the one that Amelia Earhart produced in 1912:

My goal: To fly a plane from Canada to Ireland by 1928

1. Watch pilots practicing.
2. Meet someone who has a plane.
3. Sit in a plane.
4. Ask someone to let me fly with them.
5. Practice flying with someone else.
6. Get a pilot's license.
7. Practice flying alone.

8. Study a map of Canada and decide on a route to fly.
9. Fly the route with someone.
10. Fly a longer route.
11. Fly it alone.
12. Get sponsorship for flight across the Atlantic.
13. Acquire a great plane.
14. Decide upon the route.
15. Think of all the things that might go wrong.
16. Talk to someone who has already done it.
17. Have a contingency plan in case things do go wrong.
18. Tell the press.
19. Tell the American Embassy.
20. Fly across the ocean.

There would be many more on Amelia's list, but you get the gist. And don't skimp. Time spent on preparing pays a dividend.

If you would like to find out more about preparation listen to my interview with Etienne Stott on the "I DID YOU CAN" podcast series. At the age of 32 Etienne and his partner Tim Baillie won the Gold medal in canoe slalom at the 2012 London Olympics. Just let that sink in. Olympic Gold. So many dream of such a success. But Etienne got there. "Was it ecstasy or relief?" I asked him. "Satisfaction" he replied.

Etienne grew up in Bedford. He had been a committed kayaker from his early teenage years and by 15 was running twice a week and was on the water at least three times a week. He also took his school studies seriously so there was a lot of pressure on him. Etienne was driven from that early stage by imagining himself on the rostrum with a Gold medal being placed around his neck. It mattered so much to him. His preparation for what lay ahead was spread across almost 20 years.

He did well enough in his A level studies to earn a place on an Engineering course at Nottingham University. It had to be Nottingham because it was close to the National Watersports Centre. Etienne was so committed to his sport that he avoided the normal social life of a university student in favour of training and competition. Still more preparation. It really mattered to him. By then he had become a canoe slalom specialist and had partnered with Tim. Successes followed quite frequently but there were setbacks too.

2008 was to be the big year. The Olympics were to be held in Beijing, China and all the evidence suggested Etienne would be there. But he wasn't. He failed to qualify. And he was desolate. When you've staked everything upon achieving a goal and it has slipped away it must be so difficult to get back on track. In 2011 when London was in sight he dislocated his shoulder and once more it looked as if everything he had sacrificed in order to achieve his goal might be in vain. However, with the aid of fitness specialists, psychologists and coaches Etienne and Tim were selected for the 2012 team. Despite only qualifying for the final as the 6th fastest pair they managed to surge to the Gold Medal. The challenge was complete but the effort that Etienne expended was extraordinary. Could he have prepared better? It's hard to see how.

Etienne has now set himself an even bigger challenge. He volunteers for Extinction Rebellion because he wants to raise the profile of the dangers presented by global warming. He appreciates that what they do might not always be popular but is willing to do what it takes to ensure future generations are able to enjoy a clean, healthy planet on which to live. This is his current challenge and, of course, he researches, meets others, arranges events, writes. He prepares.

I climbed Kilimanjaro - and learnt things.

Scan for the full interview with Etienne.

My Kilimanjaro tips about preparing well are :

- Preparation is essential. If you try to paint a room without sanding down the woodwork, covering the carpets and buying the right paint things won't end well. The preparation might not be glamorous but without it the challenge won't be met.

- Lack of preparation is not likely to lead you to triumph. Spend time thinking about what you hope to achieve. Carry out research. Find others who have done something similar and learn from them.

- *"Give me six hours to chop down a tree and I will spend the first four sharpening the axe,"* said Abraham Lincoln. I can see his point. More time will be spent on the preparation than on the final act. Be ready for action.

Philip Crompton

Life lesson 3: Network- nicely!

"Every friend starts out as a stranger".

Terri Nakamura

I was excited about the prospect of meeting other people on the trip to Tanzania. Meeting people always seems like a chance to enhance my life. Other people are different. They have different experiences, personalities, and lifestyles. We can always learn from each other. And of course, we can help each other. Networking matters.

I took every opportunity to find out as much as possible about the other members of our Kilimanjaro party. Everyone has a back story and in no time, I had discovered that Chad was a blood bank manager who was aiming to get to the highest point of every one of the states of the USA. Sophie managed a logistics operation in Melbourne, Laura worked for the confectionary company Mars and had a boyfriend who had his own electrician business and Vicky was a Canadian who had moved to Australia to be with her boyfriend and was training to become a counsellor. Laura from Wexford worked for eBay and had a partner who lived in Cork whilst Iggy from Norway had been working in a nursery and had travelled extensively. Dan and Emma were a recently married couple. He was from Quorn near Loughborough, and she was from Surrey. They had met through their work with Adidas, lived in Germany and were coming to the end of a 6-month honeymoon. Dan was Ian's son. Ian I knew well enough beforehand- key points: married, 4 children, retired from corporate life, Chair of Governors at a school, Chair of a Netball club, a former athlete and co-owner of a spaniel.

Once you have that sort of information it is easy to gauge how to converse with others. There's common ground. It's a long time since I read "How to Win Friends and Influence People" by Dale Carnegie. It's an international best seller for a reason. It's considered a work of genius. He was something of a trailblazer. Little wonder that Carnegie had sold out events across the USA in the 1930's as he shared his wisdom. There was a gap in the market and the population recognised this.

I will not spend too much time on what Carnegie's messages were but do consider reading it. A piece that sticks with me is the section titled "6 ways to make people like you", which includes the following:-

1. Become genuinely interested in other people.

2. Smile.

3. Remember that a person's name is to that person the sweetest and most important sound in any language.

4. Be a good listener. Encourage others to talk about themselves.

5. Talk in terms of the other person's interests.

6. Make the other person feel important- and do it sincerely".

Simple but beautiful!

The importance of networking came to me relatively late in life. I had often heard the mantra *"It's not what you know, it's who you know"* and had considered it a limiter. And let's face it, if you are brought up in a village in the industrial northwest of England there are certain restrictions. Who did I know who would open doors for me? Whilst I had a happy childhood, I rarely came into social contact with someone who worked in an office, a school, a bank, or a hospital. My ears weren't hearing the language that was used in middle class England nor were my eyes fully open to the myriad of opportunities that existed in the world.

I went to a Grammar School but still found myself socialising with those from working class worlds who holidayed in Scarborough and Blackpool - if they holidayed at all. Who spoke with Lancashire accents and rarely, if ever, used words with more than 3 syllables. And whose parents worked for the National Coal Board, Wigan Council and Pilkington's Glass or were self-employed plumbers, electricians, or builders. Let me be clear, I am not complaining nor am I being patronising. These were often interesting people who led decent lives. I merely emphasise these points to show how distant, at that point, were the careers and lifestyles that I later found myself surrounded by. My parents didn't socialise for betterment. They had friends, relatives, and work colleagues who they met up with because they had something in common and enjoyed their company. I took that with me for years and hope I still do but I also grew to appreciate the importance of having a wide range of contacts, associates and, yes, friends.

I have continued to enjoy the company of the type of people I was brought up with. I wish that was true of everyone. There is no hiding from the fact that our society is riddled with snobbery. Some people look down on others. Others are in awe of people who are apparently above them in our ludicrous social hierarchy. I hope I am guilty of neither. I remain a big supporter of the actor Jimmy Durante's creed:

"You had better be nice to people on the way up because you'll probably meet them again on the way down."

By the time I was in my late 30's, the penny had dropped. I was not going to join a society such as the Freemasons (a semi-secret society that offers support to like-minded people), but I would search out connection with people from different backgrounds. For one, they would open my mind and secondly, they just might be useful for any projects I had in mind. In truth I took a bit of a scattergun approach. I just like meeting new people. Perhaps the most effective networkers take a strategic view of what they would like to achieve, highlight those who might provide leverage and work out how to meet these potential influencers.

People pay for this stuff.

When I discovered that many private schools have lessons in networking I was amazed. I had never experienced anything approaching a networking lesson. I did try to improve such provision at the schools that I led but other pressures always meant they were on the back burner and, almost inevitably, likely to be ignored by most OFSTED inspectors.

A website I found helping parents to select a school for their children says that private schools networking systems generally:

- *Build self-confidence.*

- *Advance communication skills*

- *Make connections for future careers that will last.*

- *Gain fresh industry knowledge*

- *Gain advice and insight into potential future careers*

- *Raise your profile when applying for jobs.*

The same website says :

"Networking is a significant part of a private education which is wholly missing in the state sector. Warminster School in Wiltshire, for example, holds regular events where it's students can mix with influential people.

State schools do not tend to have the kind of contacts which would be required to organize such events."

So networking, communication and making contacts can change a life. Who would have thought it? Private schools boast about their awareness of it, yet no government has considered networking important enough to make it compulsory and thereby equip the other 93% of the population with such skills. Some private schools have very well-established networking systems. Eton College now has an online package available for sale to share some of their secrets about engaging with others whilst Repton School's inspection report (not OFSTED by the way) notes:

"Pupils are highly articulate communicators who speak confidently with their peers and adults."

and

"Pupils have high levels of self-confidence and are consequently very well prepared for life after they leave school".

The inspection report later says:-

"..........the school explicitly develops these skills, for example in house and school debates, and in a public speaking course taken by all pupils in the sixth form. Pupils use these debating skills well in lessons."

But if you can't or won't pay.....

93% of the UK population is not directly educated in networking. We pick it up as we go along. What a disadvantage. Opportunities must emerge but they pass us by because we aren't able to mix with the right people.

You might have heard of "Six degrees of separation". This emerged from a short story by Frigyes Karinthy and argues that we are just six handshakes away from everyone else. So, I am in theory able to contact the President of the United States through a maximum of six introductions. I thought it through and realised that my world had been distorted for a while because I had met former Chancellor of the Exchequer Kenneth Clarke on a few occasions. He could probably lead me to President Biden very rapidly, maybe directly. Just 2 handshakes

When you start to think like that it's amazing how easy networking seems. I'm not saying that the President would be excited to hear from me- in truth he would probably delete any message or bin any letter- but it shows what can be done and if you make a suggestion, offer a compliment, or share an idea then who knows? And you don't have to aim quite so far. Contact with your local MP, a business owner or journalist ought to be easy enough to set up. Give it a go. Get known.

I have a group of friends from university days. We meet up every 5 years or so in Hull- well, we did attend university there and developed a bond with the place. At the re-union dinner we play a game. Who is the most famous person you have met in the last 5 years? Guy mixes with lots of famous cricketers and could win quite easily most years. In fairness to the rest of us he keeps Flintoff, Stokes, and Root out of his contributions. I was particularly excited one year because I had briefly established a link with the then Tottenham footballer and now BBC presenter Jermaine Jenas. An ace in the pack surely. Well...... a new person had joined us for the first time. John was the CEO of a multi-national. It was suggested that he went first and after a little thought said:

"I was at Davos (a major economic summit) and sat at the same table as Ban-Ki Moon (Secretary General of the United Nations), Vice President John Kerry and Bill Gates." I put Jermaine away for use on another day. Some people are way ahead in the networking stakes.

I should say that you may not want to network in the most obvious sense. Collecting influential names might appal you. I understand that. But at least consider pulling together like-minded people into a small network. You might be united by a hobby, a job, family circumstances or a news story. It usually helps to open your mind and explore ideas with others.

On Kilimanjaro, there was no link to either Wi-Fi or mobile phone networks. That meant that everyone was detached from Facebook, Instagram, Twitter, TikTok, LinkedIn and WhatsApp. I don't think that anyone suffered withdrawal symptoms, but conversation did include reference to each of the different apps and how it helped or hindered lives. There was agreement that each could be entertaining in its way and that it could be interesting to find out what was happening and how people were making each other smile. No harm in that. There were concerns that hours could pass as you scrolled through item after item. And neither you nor the world was any the better by the end of the lost hours. We agreed that time restrictions were ideal and that focusing upon one app would be sensible.

If I were to be so bold as to offer advice to someone looking to make their way in the world I suggest: -

1. Have a LinkedIn page and follow people who are of significance in your chosen world. Say nice things about what they post- if you think they deserve it. Everyone has an ego. Make sure that your 'bio page' presents you as someone pleasant to work with.

2. Have a couple of work-related WhatsApp groups. Don't post anything controversial but do occasionally back up someone else if they say something just a little different.

3. Use Instagram or X (it'll always be Twitter to me) for connection with the outside world but follow people who you might not obviously agree with. An open mind has merits.

4. Use Facebook for family and close friends but do control who has you as a Friend. The system is just waiting to pull you down rabbit holes.

5. And TikTok? Not a clue what to advise there.

And if you spend more than an hour a day on social media you are doing something horribly wrong. NB. My wife avoids it completely. She has several WhatsApp groups but draws a line there. Her life is none the worse for this. Nowadays I'm only on X because I like to be kept up to date about the latest dramas surrounding my football team. There are plenty of them.

PS. I suspect nobody will listen to my advice about social media!

If you want to find out more about networking check out my interview with John Fallon in the "I DID YOU CAN" podcast series. *John was the CEO of the international publishing company Pearson for 8 years and worked within the organisation for 20. It was a high-profile, well-paid role which involved a lot of foreign travel, thousands of meetings, many decisions, and a huge weight of responsibility. And it wasn't something that the 14-year-old John ever considered as a possible way of life when he was growing up in north Manchester. In fact, the only dream he had at that stage was to play football for Manchester City.*

John's father was a primary school headteacher and his mother was a teaching assistant. His grandfather was born to an unmarried mother in late nineteenth century Ireland. As a result, he was brought up in a home run by the nuns. As John said, "He would never have believed that his grandson would lead a major company". There was no history of business acumen in the family. John was pretty much self-taught.

John did reasonably well at school but was quiet and invisible. There was nothing to suggest what lay ahead. It was at Hull University that he started to emerge as the person I have got to know in recent years. He had realised that at 18 he could create something of a new identity for himself and in no time was at the heart of student politics, writing for the student newspaper and part of the university football team. He became more confident as he met new people and met with some success. He was networking. Was he meeting people just to ease his was through society? No. He likes people. By the time he was 21 John was President of the Student Union and in his address book was the future Deputy Prime Minister John Prescott. It is hard to deny that such a contact was helpful.

After he left university John worked in Public Relations for Gateshead Council before being enticed into the political world as a researcher for Mr. Prescott MP. He was absorbed by political life, and it seemed that he might be tempted to carve out a career in Westminster. However, he saw a post working within the Pearson empire, applied for it, and moved through the ranks waving goodbye to Parliament.

Once he started work in the business world, he showed he was prepared to work hard and take on challenges that others were wary of. He also had communication skills which attracted the attention of senior managers and was eventually asked if he would be the CEO. He had been ill so turned down the opportunity at first. The idea of spending more time with his family appealed but when he was asked again, he said "yes".

I climbed Kilimanjaro - and learnt things.

The interview with John shows what can be achieved with the right mindset. John Fallon at 14 never gave a thought to a career at the top of a major business. The slightly older version has found huge satisfaction through meeting new people, developing relationships, taking risks, and making a difference. Check John out on **"I DID YOU CAN"**. *He's inspiring.*

Scan for the full interview with John.

My Kilimanjaro tips about networking nicely are:

- Enjoy the company of other people. If you get a reputation for being a decent, interested person it is amazing how others will be prepared to help you.

- Do not restrict your interest in people to those who are at the top of the hierarchy. So often I hear stories of how the best leaders show interest in everyone. Sir Alex Ferguson, the highly successful manager of Manchester United, famously knew the names of cleaners and catering staff as well as the players and the executives. It bought him a lot of goodwill.

- If someone does something that seems worthy of praise, then congratulate them or thank them. Nobody wants to be seen as the 'class creep' but if your boss or a potentially influential person says or does something that you admire consider sending a note or saying something positive. Don't overdo it of course!

- Use social media …. a bit. But be careful. The more you contribute the more potential mistakes you can make. Some people are easily offended and an innocent phrase or 'like' might cause you problems.

Life lesson 4: Challenge yourself to do great things.

"You are never too old to set another goal or dream a new dream".

C.S. Lewis

Climbing Kilimanjaro was certainly a challenge. I chose to take it on. Sometimes you find yourself facing a challenge that you didn't choose. It might be an illness, a financial problem, something work-related or a bereavement. So many things happen in life. You either work through them or give up. Usually, we battle on. We move up the mountain.

It's sensible to set your own challenges. They keep you limbered up for the ones that are forced upon you but also help you to develop as a person. And we can set our own challenges at any stage of life.

Miley Cyrus- I'm a big fan- has a song called 'The Climb.' I used it a lot at school presentations. It's all about the importance of dealing with challenge. It's not Shakespeare but it gets across a simple message beautifully. Life is often tough, and it's never done. The challenges just keep on coming and you have to keep on dealing with them. I kept humming it as I moved slowly to the summit of Kilimanjaro.

Here are some of the lyrics :-

"I can almost see it
That dream I'm dreaming, but
There's a voice inside my head saying
"You'll never reach it"
Every step I'm taking
Every move I make feels lost with no direction
My faith is shaken

But I, I gotta keep trying
Gotta keep my head held high.

There's always gonna be another mountain
I'm always gonna wanna make it move
Always gonna be an uphill battle
Sometimes I'm gonna have to lose
Ain't about how fast I get there
Ain't about what's waiting on the other side
It's the climb "

When I returned to the UK from Africa, a number of people asked, "What's next then?" My initial reaction was to say "That's me done. I'm happy with the quiet life now. I'll walk the dog and cut the grass." But of course, that soon changed. Life can't be like that. Not for me and I guess if you have read this far then not for you either.

If we accept that climb follows climb, then we need to be equipped with the skills and the traits necessary to ensure we aren't daunted by what we are experiencing and what is to come. In this book I have already described the climb that I took part in. A team of people came together because they wanted to get to the top of the biggest mountain in Africa. Each member of the team had different motivations, different pasts, strengths, and weaknesses. The first part of the book told the story from day to day. How far we ascended. What we saw. Some of the things people said. This part is, of course, dealing with the lessons learned during The Climb. You might want to play Miley Cyrus in the background as we consider how Kilimanjaro influenced me and how I suggest you might deal with the challenges you will inevitably face as you try to fulfil your potential and, as the American philosopher David Thoreau said, *"Live the life you imagined."*

Try the 'Wheel of Life'

There's something called 'The Wheel of Life' that coaches employ. It's simple really. A circle is divided into 6 different sections. Each relates to an aspect of your life. So, for example: Paid employment, exercise, family, holidays, volunteering, learning. You give each a mark out of 10 to indicate how satisfied you are with it and then join the marks together on the divided circle. It might look something like this.

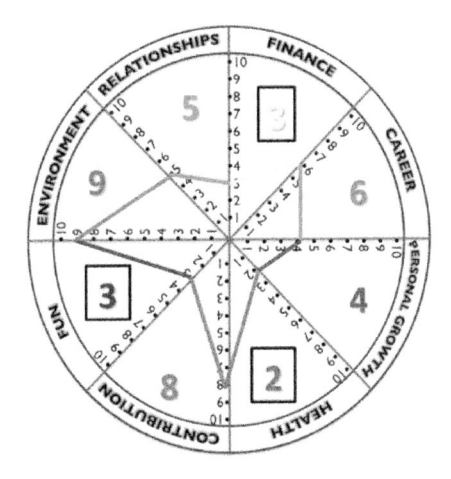

The Wheel opens discussion and makes points from which goals should emerge. It would appear that the person who completed this wheel might need to focus upon their health before anything else. 2 out of 10 is disturbingly low. A conversation about their health might conclude that exercise, diet, or visits to professionals need addressing with specific goals emerging. Anything that helps focus the mind is useful. Focussing on too many things at any one time is doomed to be less successful. I am a victim of this. So many things seem important, but the more your time is divided the less the impact on any one thing. The wonder of Kilimanjaro was that only one thing mattered for that week: To climb the mountain.

Coaches often return to the wheel in subsequent sessions in order to consider if the work completed so far has made a difference and to agree new goals.

It would be worth you carrying out a similar piece of thinking using the wheel below as a guide. Add any labels that suit you. Perhaps these are helpful prompts: Career, Relationships, Fun, Excitement, Exercise, Volunteering, Holidays, Money.....

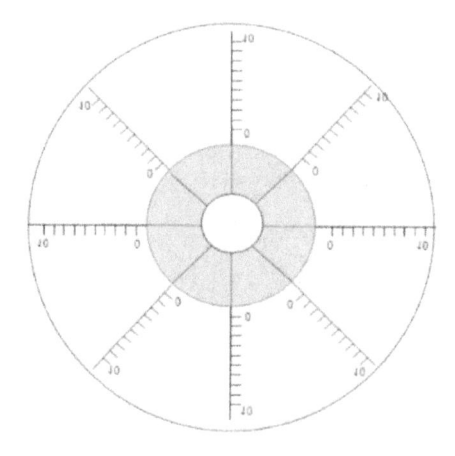

Once you have reflected upon the appearance of the wheel you will be clearer as to what sort of challenge (or goal) you need to set yourself.

Some of my challenges

Challenges come in many forms. Here are some I have set myself either formally or informally over the years. I present this list not to boast. A significant number of them have ended unsuccessfully but occasionally- when I did things properly - things worked out well. Again, I refer you to my podcast series **"I DID YOU CAN"** which shows that all sorts of people face all sorts of challenges.

I climbed Kilimanjaro - and learnt things.

Here are some of mine:-

1. To run the London Marathon in less than 4 hours: *Did it in 2000.*
2. To become a chartered accountant. *Bad choice. Not thought through.*
3. To recover from Guillain Barre Syndrome. *Took me 6 months but I did it- with a lot of help from my friends.*
4. To be a Headteacher by the time I was 40: *Did it. I had a plan.*
5. To lead a school from 'inadequate' to 'good'. *Did it in 2006. Plan in place.*
6. To write a book. *Did it in 2019 with "In Search of My Alumni".*
7. To play tennis well. *Failed. Gave it 2 years then hurt shoulder. Gave up.*
8. To speak French well. *Far from it. Had a plan but put it on a shelf.*
9. To train a spaniel. *Work in progress. No plan. He's beyond planning.*
10. To climb Kilimanjaro. *Did it in 2023.*

There are dozens more. What a mixed bag. Some of these challenges are short term. You identify it. Get on with it and a few months later it's either done or it's not. Kilimanjaro falls into that category.

Others may take a couple of years. Training a spaniel is definitely in that category.

Others are life works. Being a dad is never done but you keep reviewing and desperately hoping for positive feedback. Hint, hint!

Some are ways of living. They incorporate the values that are important to you. Optimism and friendliness I venture to suggest are mine. They would be on my shield if I went to war in medieval times.

Challenges ahead

For the purpose of this book, we will focus upon Kilimanjaro style challenges. I would define those as challenges that you do not necessarily need to do, that might cause discomfort, but which will bring satisfaction and help you to become a more confident person. I'm well into my 60's and continue to wonder what I might do next. What challenge awaits? There are plenty around. Occasionally I think it would be nice to just look after the garden, walk the dog and listen to Radio 4. I respect those who are at peace with that. I'm just too aware of the energy that I have. I want to use it for my own satisfaction but also to make a positive impact upon the world.

I am going to get the quotation at the start of this section printed onto a T shirt.

"You are never too old to set another goal or dream a new dream" C.S. Lewis

Thanks C.S!

An interesting exercise is to consider what people might say about you when they meet up in 10 years' time. I'm reluctant to say "at your funeral" but it is of course a possibility. Let's imagine there's a conversation in a bar and someone mentions your name. What words might be used? How about this:

*"What a great person. Not only were they a wonderful plumber who went out of their way to ensure customers were looked after but also helped to raise money every year for a children's charity. I remember when they helped cook Christmas dinner for 30 homeless people. No one could have looked after a parent like * did. It was almost saintly. And then that book they wrote about their family. That was amazing. And have you seen the*

garden? It's incredible. Must have taken so much time and I know that until the last 5 years or so they knew nothing about gardening. "

You get the idea.

This is what I **wouldn't** want people to say about me.

"Phil was a very poor headteacher. I know people who said it was dreadful working for him. But he was always at work and never spent much time with his family. He's got grandchildren in London but hardly ever helps. That dog of his is bonkers. It never does as it's told, and Phil gets so cross with it. He does the parkrun, but his time gets worse every week. He needs to lose weight. Too many cakes and beers. No wonder he pulled out of that crazy plan to cycle the length of the country. He's got a campervan and goes to France now and again. Heaven knows how he copes because his French is awful. He's got a big garden but it's a right mess. The rest of the village must be embarrassed at the state of it. I don't know who he is friends with. People seem to come along and then disappear. It's little wonder. Oh, and that plan to climb Kilimanjaro came to nothing. He made it through the first 2 days I hear and then gave up. Typical. And the book that he wrote about it. How boring? How unhelpful. He gave up supporting that football team too just because they got relegated."

I think we would agree that there's a lot to work at. This is what I **would** like people to say about me.

"Phil was a really good headteacher. I know people who said he was great to work for. But he always put his family first. Still does. He's always helping with the grandchildren in London. And that spaniel. When he first got him, it was crazy but now he's good as gold. Phil was so patient with him. I'm amazed that he was able to get his parkrun time below 23 minutes. That's some going. And he cycled from Land's End to John o Groats. Incredible. He had to lose a lot of weight to make that happen. Every year he goes to France with that campervan, and I'm told his French is really good now. And that garden ! Everyone in his village said how beautiful it looks. Phil's still got friends from all stages of his life. That says a lot, I think. I remember when he said he was going to climb Kilimanjaro I thought he was too old. He must have been 63 but he did it and raised money for that cycling charity. I loved that book he wrote about it. It wasn't just about the climb; it was about what he learned from the experience. No wonder it went to the top of the best seller lists. And he carried on supporting Wigan Athletic despite everything. "

If number 1 is to be avoided and number 2 achieved, then challenges need to be set and met. (The work-related stuff is in the past. It's not possible to change that)

1. Train the dog properly.

2. Get fit enough to run a 5km parkrun in 22 minutes 59 seconds or less.

3. Start riding my bike regularly again.

4. Hire a French tutor.

5. Do more with my garden beyond cutting the grass.

6. Make sure this book is the best it can be by asking others to read it before publishing.

7. Lose at least 5 kilograms in weight.

8. Renew my football season ticket.

9. Email a few old friends who I've lost touch with.

10. Book in some visits to London to see the family.

10 challenges. All doable. Lands' End to John o' Groats is a very big doubt at the moment but the Harvard Business School in 2005 encouraged us to **"Create a big dream".**

Setting the challenge

The Kilimanjaro experience was a two-part challenge:

1. To climb to the top of the mountain.

2. To write a book about the climb.

In order to complete challenges, it is important to consider the need to set good clear goals. Kilimanjaro was very clear. When in July 2022 Ian first asked me about my availability this is the plan I should have written:-

"To climb Mount Kilimanjaro in February 2023."

- To ensure my weight is below 90kg by Feb 2023
- To have walked 10 kms in hilly terrain on 5 consecutive days by January 2023
- To have walked slowly up Mount Snowdon between midnight and 7.00am by December 2022.
- To have acquired essential kit by Feb 2023.
- To book flights by November 2022
- To get visas by December 2022

Now that's a goal. Clear and thorough. I managed to get to the top of Kilimanjaro, but it would probably have been more straightforward if I had truly committed to the actions. I was probably a bit too heavy, maybe towards the end of the hike I was wearier than expected, climbing at night would have prepared my head for what was to come, there would have been less of a rush getting the kit together, we might have booked better flights and the stress associated with the visas would have been reduced with a bit more planning.

Earhart, Curie, Bannister, Hillary, Tensing, MacArthur, and Ederle were the sort of people who moved from challenge to challenge. In a much smaller way, I hope I have too. I have friends who have embraced far more challenges than me. Far more. I have other friends who have been content with living quieter lives within their comfort zones. They tend the roses, go to church, walk the dog, carry on working into their 70's and travel the length of the country watching a football team. They are content doing the things they have always done. As I trekked up and down Kilimanjaro, I once again realised that there is no right way to live this life, but I am convinced that knowing yourself and what is likely to make you feel satisfied is crucial. And if you can do that without setting at least one personal challenge I would be amazed.

If you want to find out more about a person who has challenged themselves then check out my interview with Jacqui Callan on the podcast series "I DID YOU CAN". When Jacqui was 14, she wondered if she might become a lawyer but decided that a girl from a working-class background in Warrington, Cheshire was not likely to achieve anything quite so illustrious. So, she set the bar a bit lower, made it to university and studied Social Studies. She took the course seriously and started to blossom academically but also took on some challenging work experiences that included shifts at a Derby Secure Unit, probation service *work in her hometown of Warrington and further probation work in Leicestershire. By the time she graduated she was in demand and became the youngest ever probation officer to be appointed in Leicestershire. Jacqui thrived in the role and took on more and more projects that really tested her.*

By the time she was 31 Jacqui was married with a young family but had realised that barristers were using the reports she had written to enhance their own careers. The dream of a 14-year-old was perhaps more achievable than she had imagined. Lawyers weren't necessarily super talented she decided. They were just people who believed in themselves and worked hard. So, Jacqui gave up her job as a probation officer and studied to become a solicitor. When she qualified, she was so pleased. Goal reached. But then came the work that was required to be a successful Criminal Defence solicitor. Any thoughts of a 9-5 life soon disappeared, and she found herself busy most days, evenings, and weekends. Holidays would be interrupted by calls. She believed strongly that everyone should be properly represented when accused of a crime. It didn't feel like a peaceful life, but she loved it. It felt like her destiny. Soon Jacqui was overseeing cases between Newcastle and Truro along with just one other qualified solicitor and a team of para-legals. In Court Jacqui felt on equal terms with barristers, lawyers, and judges. They respected her because they knew her backstory- one that illustrated determination, diligence, and drive at all stages. She was also very good at what she did.

Today Jacqui's work involves defending medical professionals who have been accused of crimes and need to be defended. She is at the gym on a stationary bike by 6.00am every day and deals with e-mails as she pedals. Life is full on, but Jacqui finds it so satisfying. She has faced many challenges and overcome them.

Philip Crompton

Scan to hear the full interview with Jacqui.

My Kilimanjaro tips about challenging yourself to do great things are:

- Complete the wheel and identify the areas you feel least happy with and from there set a challenge. Write it down. Break the challenge into a goal – or goals.

- Check your progress towards the goal. What will you have achieved? By when? If you aren't where you want to be ask yourself why not and adapt the plan.

- Don't underestimate yourself. Human beings have shown they can do extraordinary things. They have even landed on the Moon! Why can't you get to that metaphorical Venus? This is particularly relevant for those from backgrounds which have not exposed them to high profile jobs. If you stand back others with less talent but more confidence just might step in. And then what?

Life lesson 5: Be a team player.

"Alone we can do so little, together we can do so much".

Helen Keller

It would have been possible I guess, to climb Kilimanjaro alone. No doubt many people have. Being part of a team made it so much easier. There were two teams that merged into one. The team that had paid for the experience consisted of ten people from around the world. 6 women, 4 men. The eldest was 63, the youngest 24. The tallest was 6 feet 3 inches, the shortest was 5 feet and 0 inches. They were from 6 different countries. 2 were parents, 1 was a grandparent. They were united by one challenge – to get to the top of Mount Kilimanjaro. The power of a shared challenge. That's what helps to create a great team.

Alongside the team of tourists was a band of brothers – and one sister. They were the team that eased our way to the summit. So many different things needed to be done. There was all the stuff that had to be carried on heads and backs from camp to camp: personal luggage, tents, food - and a toilet. Tents had to be erected and dismantled, food had to be cooked and served, water was collected from sometimes distant streams and support had to be provided for ailing participants. And then there was the leadership of the venture. More of that later.

So often on the trip, I was moved by the power of teams. People working together to complete a challenge, to reach a goal.

At night, my mind often wandered to teams in which I had played a role There were school football teams that I had been part of. Occasionally successful, sometimes disastrous, and usually just enjoyable. And then the teams I had played for in my 20's and 30's. A similar patchwork. My brief experience as an accountant saw small teams pulled together for a week or so. As a teacher I was part of departmental and year teams as well as the whole school team. Some worked well, some didn't. And the family team. Such an important part of my life. Teams are everywhere. Making them work is so important.

In my leadership role, I frequently referred to the words of the American anthropologist Margaret Mead:

"Never doubt that a small group of committed citizens can change the world; indeed, it's the only thing that ever has".

I think the quote made a difference. I was asked to take over a school that inspectors judged to be in need of what OFSTED calls "Special Measures". There was a darkness around the place, but it had many good teachers and hundreds of children who deserved a better experience. At my first meeting with the staff team, I showed a picture of a sailing ship being tossed around on a brutal, grey sea with rain lashing down. Underneath was the caption "Fair Wind, Full Sail." I found it in the National Maritime Museum in Falmouth the week before I took up the role. The poster struck a chord, and I followed it up with Margaret's quote. Suddenly – and I don't use that word lightly- there seemed to be a different atmosphere in the school. There was something to aim for. A challenge with a goal. Everyone knew they had a part to play and what that part was.

Teams need clarity and an agreed target because otherwise the blurring of edges means that frustration and irritation can kick in. A ship needs to know precisely where it is aiming for. Without a clear destination it can move south then east then northwest and then back to the south. And it gets nowhere. Being part of a team that sailed from "Special Measures" to "Good" in record time was the most satisfying experience of my career. It was wonderful to see capable teachers and leaders blossom as they appreciated knowing clearly what their jobs were and how they were progressing towards our target.

I really ought to resist but I can't. The most exhilarating day of my life was May 11th, 2013. It was the day that Wigan Athletic beat Manchester City in the FA Cup Final. I had supported 'little Wigan' since the mid 1960's. I used to go to matches with my dad when they were a non-league team and have remained loyal to the cause despite living over 100 miles away from the town for the best part of 40 years. And that day was wonderful. Roberto Martinez the manager had somehow managed to convince an injury ravaged team that victory was inevitable. They were to play the current Premiership champions, a team that included some of the biggest names in world football: Yaya Toure, David Silva, Vincent Company, Carlos Tevez. Honourable defeat was what Wigan supporters hoped for. But the team had a higher aim.

There were lots of symbols that were used to create a team spirit. As the players walked into the dressing room there was a huge sign saying 'Believe'. The team used a system which Martinez had only rarely used before and that must have excited the players, the fans had a song "I'm a Believer" by The Monkees and this created unity, the team was led out onto the pitch by owner and proud Wiganer Dave Whelan and the captain Emmerson Boyce carried a little disabled boy in his arms as he walked onto the Wembley turf. All ideas that pulled the team together. Manchester City had most of the talent but none of the unity and, remarkably, Wigan scored in the last minute of the match to win the FA Cup. What an achievement.

I wrote the last paragraph with goosebumps. This was partly because I was remembering a day almost exactly 10 years ago when my little team beat a monster - but also because of my belief in the power of teamwork.

Much has been written about teamwork. I particularly like these 8 characteristics of a successful team which are taken from https://skillpath.com/blog/effective-teamwork :-

1. People who are on a team know they are dependent on each other. They understand that personal and team goals are important. By realizing this, time and effort aren't wasted squabbling and achieving personal gain at the expense of others.

2. When individuals work as part of a team, they work in an atmosphere of trust and are encouraged to express themselves openly. This type of environment encourages team members to ask questions and be more creative in solving problems.

3. Team members feel ownership for their jobs and team because they have made a personal investment into the team. They focus on being successful for the team's sake more than being part of a group.

4. Teams encourage individual members to apply their individual talent and knowledge to team objectives; thus, members contribute to the organization's success.

5. All team members practice open communication with each other. They ensure they understand each other. This helps to foster a climate of trust among the team members.

6. Great teams encourage members to learn on the job and develop new skills. Teams support members that want to learn and become more efficient.

7. Decision-making involves the entire team. However, they understand that the team leader will decide if they cannot find a solution.

8. Good teams resolve conflicts quickly and constructively. Team members are comfortable being open with each other and communicate freely.

I'm at ease with all those but would add:-

9. They have symbols and language that unite them as a team.

10. They celebrate success.

The older I get, the more I have become convinced that teams make the difference. Major changes that happen have a group of people united around a cause. They share a commitment to make something happen.

My friend Alison lives in Cornwall and is currently part of a group that is determined to showcase a new musical. The musical has a writer, there are actors, musicians, scenery creators, fund raisers. Just by talking to her, I realised how passionate the team is. It will happen.

The classic story of successful teamwork involves the project to land Apollo 11 on the Moon in 1969. It is estimated that 400,000 people had a role in the 'super team'. This involved scientists, technicians, engineers, administrators, cooks, maintenance staff and, famously, the janitors. Legend has it that the systems to engage everyone in the project were so effective that, when President John Kennedy had visited the NASA base in 1962, he met a whole range of staff. At one point he was talking to a janitor, unaware of his role. When asked "And what do you do here?" the man responded, "I'm helping to put a man on the moon". And of course, he was. It's the perfect story of making everyone feel valuable.

I think it is also worth dwelling upon what a bad team looks like.

The latter days of Boris Johnson's government is a good example. For months, the rest of the Cabinet appeared to be scheming to get him to leave Number 10 Downing Street. To be fair to them, they probably had good reason. It looked awful. Some people threatened to resign, and then others actually did. They cited concerns about parties held at the Prime Minister's residence during the Covid lockdown period, the leader's response to a colleague's apparent inappropriate sexual behaviour, the PM seeming to 'mislead' the House of Commons……. They just kept coming. When Chancellor Rishi Sunak and Health Secretary Sajid Javid resigned on the same day it was clearly all over for Team Johnson. For months, they had lost sight of their goal i.e. to run the country properly and had degenerated to a group that clearly neither liked nor respected each other. At the very highest level, a team failed, leaving many to wonder if the Government truly is the highest level.

I am typing as another football season comes to an end. Chelsea have had a miserable time. Their new owners have changed their manager 3 times and signed countless players for many millions of pounds. Apparently, they had to increase the size of the dressing room to accommodate the squad. Most of the players knew they would not feature in the next match day squad, and this will have created disgruntlement and cliques. Each manager would have forlornly tried to get the team to focus upon the challenge ahead and none of the three had any success. It gave the appearance of chaos. A team can be too big, not have sufficient commitment to their leader and feel strong enough to undermine both the manager and their fellow players.

And the other big story of the moment is the collapse of the ITV show "This Morning". A team that was apparently functioning so well collapsed very quickly. Frankly, I neither know nor care much about the detail. It all seems a bit trivial – though admittedly not to those embroiled in it. Essentially Phillip Schofield and Holly Willoughby fell out. It seems Phillip was keeping secrets from the other and his behaviour led to trust breaking down. I won't dwell on it, but teams can fall apart. The main goal can be lost as individuals within the team squabble. And one squabble can bring the rest of the show tumbling down.

Dr Meredith Belbin carried out research at hundreds of companies in the 1960's and 70's. He realised that the best teams included people who could cover some key roles. Just like an orchestra needs string, brass and percussion sections, a rock band needs a guitarist, bass player, drummer and a vocalist and rugby teams struggle without wingers, half backs and prop forwards so organisational teams need people in key roles. I have made use of Belbin's work to create the table below. I have assigned the name of one of the Kilimanjaro team to each of the roles. Obviously, my knowledge of the personalities involved is limited but they all seemed to like a smile, so I don't anticipate much fury from them. It's important to note that I went for 'best fit'- I saw no sign of Emma being over critical nor Laura from Wexford being inflexible! And I hope I'm not famous for offloading work.

Role	What they do	Strengths	Possible weaknesses
Monitor evaluator (Emma)	Provides a logical eye, making impartial judgements where required and weighs up the team's options in a dispassionate way.	Sober, strategic, and discerning. Sees all options and judges accurately. Gets things done.	High standards mean can be over critical sometimes.
Specialist (Chad)	Brings in-depth knowledge of a key area to the team.	Single-minded, self-starting and dedicated. They provide specialist knowledge and skills.	Tends to contribute on a narrow front and can dwell on the technicalities.
Plant (Ian)	Tends to be highly creative and good at solving problems in unconventional ways.	Creative, imaginative, free-thinking, generates ideas and solves difficult problems.	Might ignore incidentals and may be too preoccupied to communicate effectively.

Role			
Shaper (Dan)	Provides the necessary drive to ensure that the team keeps moving and does not lose focus or momentum.	Challenging, dynamic, thrives on pressure. Has the drive and courage to overcome obstacles.	Can be prone to provocation and may sometimes offend people's feelings.
Implementer (Laura from Wexford)	Needed to plan a workable strategy and carry it out as efficiently as possible.	Practical, reliable, efficient. Turns ideas into actions and organises work that needs to be done.	Can be a bit inflexible and slow to respond to new possibilities.
Completer Finisher (Laura from Melbourne)	Most effectively used at the end of tasks to polish and scrutinise the work for errors, subjecting it to the highest standards of quality control.	Painstaking, conscientious, anxious. Searches out errors. Polishes and perfects.	Can be inclined to worry unduly, and reluctant to delegate.
Co-ordinator (Phil)	Needed to focus on the team's objectives, draw out team members and delegate work appropriately.	Mature, confident, identifies talent. Clarifies goals.	Can be seen as manipulative and might offload their own share of the work.
Team worker (Sophie)	Helps the team to gel, using their versatility to identify the work required and complete it on behalf of the team.	Co-operative, perceptive and diplomatic. Listens and averts friction.	Can be indecisive in crunch situations and tends to avoid confrontation.
Resource investigator (Iggy)	Uses their inquisitive nature to find ideas to bring back to the team.	Outgoing, enthusiastic. Explores opportunities and develops contacts.	Might be over-optimistic and can lose interest once the initial enthusiasm has passed.

Which roles are you most suited to? At different stages of my life, I have carried out each of them, but I think I was happiest when I needed to be a Co-ordinator, a Plant, or a Team worker. I could fill the other roles but when I look back those three seemed like the best fit. I was never fully at ease when I was expected to carry out the duties of a Monitor Evaluator or a Specialist. And isn't that just another aspect of the excitement of life. Everyone is different. Not better or worse than each other. Just bringing different things to the party.

That said it is wise to be aware of the different roles and to consider how you might show that you could contribute to each of them. You might have a role preference but there may be times that you are required to step in to ease a short-term team deficiency **TIP: The world has a shortage of completer finishers (it might be worth finding out how you can prove you are one)**

https://www.belbin.com/about/belbin-team-roles is very helpful. The website holds a wealth of free information. You can pay for deep analysis that Belbin Ltd can provide to help teams within organisations to thrive.

On Kilimanjaro I sensed few disagreements but of course in our team we all really just had one role- to climb and help others climb to the top of the mountain. The support team operated in a different way. It seemed to work well. The challenge was clearly communicated, and roles assigned. There was a challenge to be dealt with and everyone in the team knew what they had to do. Inevitably, there were minor, barely visible hiccoughs, but the team was strong enough to deal with them. And the mission of taking ten people to the top of Africa's highest mountain and safely back to the Hotel Stella Maris was successfully accomplished.

If you would like to find out more about team playing check out my interview with Liz Slingsby on the "I DID YOU CAN" podcast series. *Liz is an educator in the Bahamas. Every two weeks groups of young people arrive at the school to experience leadership programmes. Liz has worked there for 9 years. It's a long way from where she grew up in Leicester.*

Liz has been immersed in teamwork for as long as she can remember. Her family was the first team she was a part of. She has happy memories of working as a happy unit. Holidays by the Devon coast in a touring caravan with her two brothers and her parents stand out as wonders of her life. That's a team player for you. Similarly, her school days involved sports teams and groups of friends. Liz enjoyed working with other people. That is a very helpful trait.

Since she left home to attend university in Aberystwyth she has developed a bond with the coast. Her working life has taken her to Florida and Australia before she settled in the Bahamas. In each location she has been part of relatively small teams which have a clear purpose. In Australia Liz led treks and adventures for groups of people who had to become a team for the duration of the experience, but she also had colleagues to work with. In the Bahamas Liz has held a variety of roles within the organisation. The overall aim of the school is to equip young people with leadership skills which will help them to live satisfying lives and Liz has seen the impact the work has had. Inevitably the small group of people who make sure all goes well operate as a team with everyone knowing what their role is and being prepared to acknowledge and give feedback to colleagues.

Liz has suffered from homesickness from time to time. It's a long way from Leicester to Eleuthera (in the Bahamas), Melbourne, The Florida Keys and Aberystwyth. Always it has been through the relationships with her colleagues, her teammates that she has found herself saved. Strong teams live with people long after they have disbanded, and Liz is hugely appreciative of the warmth and camaraderie that she has experienced as a team member and they too must appreciate the energy, imagination, and flexibility that she has brought to the organizations for which she has worked.

Scan to hear the full interview with Liz.

My Kilimanjaro tips about being a team player are:

- Be clear about who does what. Identify your role and ensure that areas which merge with a colleague's are fully discussed and returned to so that friction is avoided.

- Deal with problems when they arise. There will be problems. It's inevitable. Even with the best teams. If a problem is ignored it will become more impactful. There will be resentment and possibly anger. Short-term pain might be experienced as a search for a remedy, but usually long-term peace can be built. A good manager will probably spot the difficulty but openness matters.

- It is so important to agree a shared goal. There needs to be something that pulls the team together. There needs to be something to celebrate when the goal is achieved. It might not be a party. Just a congratulatory word to the team. "We did it" might suffice.

Philip Crompton

Life lesson 6: Expect discomfort – and battle through it.

"Growth is painful. Change is painful. But nothing is more as painful as staying stuck somewhere you don't belong."

Mandy Hale

Climbing Kilimanjaro wasn't easy. In many ways the experience illustrated how a life goes. Straightforward bits, hard bits. Parts that make you laugh, parts that make you cry. Those night awakenings on the side of the mountain led me to reflect, for better and for worse, on how my life had gone. The great times, and the not-so-great times.

Any life is a journey. I know some people cringe at the use of the term. Sorry if you are one of those. To stay in one place where you feel secure, safe and in control is all very well, but you probably won't grow and at some point, may well find yourself bored. This is often called the Comfort Zone. To leave it, you need to step into the Fear Zone in which you will be affected by the opinions of others, find excuses, and lack confidence. It is truly a tough place to be and the temptation to dart back into the Comfort Zone will remain. But if you persevere, you will enter the Learning Zone in which you will acquire new skills and be able to deal with challenges. And in no time, you will be in the Growth Zone in which you will live your dreams, find purpose, and realise your aspirations. Abraham Maslow wrote in 1943:

"What a person can be they must be." (Adapted from the original focus upon one gender)

I climbed Kilimanjaro - and learnt things.

That's what leaving the Comfort Zone can deliver.

My journey through life includes the following experiences in which I experienced Comfort, Fear, Learning and Growth. Sometimes the movement was aided by others, sometimes I just motivated myself: -

- Secondary school was an often-disappointing experience. I didn't enjoy much of it. I felt like there was someone lurking inside that nobody was helping me to find. Someone eventually asked me what I wanted to do when I left school. I was 16 at the time. I said I would like to be a journalist. And that was that. Nobody encouraged me. I didn't know any journalists. I assumed it wasn't the sort of job that people like me did. I think I'd have enjoyed being a journalist.

- I went to university because when I was 14, a geography teacher called Mr. Rimmer told me that I was good at the subject. Fortunately, he taught me geography and geology at A level. If he hadn't, I suspect I would not have got the grades required and my life would have gone along a different route. One person made a difference. Just imagine if Mr. Rimmer had left the school before I arrived.

- I played football for the school and my village until I was 15. I then lost confidence because most of the other boys seemed to have hit puberty, grown taller, stronger, and acquired moustaches. I didn't play again until I was 18. I then carried on playing until I was 36. I so wish I had not stopped playing football for those three years, but confidence is a strange thing. It comes and goes.

- Hull University was great fun. I made lots of friends, laughed a lot, drank a bit too much beer and did enough studying to get by. I didn't excel. Getting to university was enough. Nobody else in my family had ever done it. I'd reached the top of my mountain. Or so I thought. Looking back my course was interesting, but it was always a sideshow. I met John Fallon a couple of years ago. He went to Hull just after me. He was active in politics, sports, and journalism whilst he was there and went on to lead a multi-national company. Perhaps I should have been similarly energised.

- After university I started to train as an accountant. I realised quickly that it wasn't for me. Such a miserable few months. To escape I applied for a place at a teacher training college. When I was accepted, I resigned from my potentially glorious career as an accountant (?) and went to the Costa Brava in Spain to run a campsite. I liked that very much. Putting up tents, chatting to holidaymakers and sunbathing suited me down to the ground. If I had known myself a bit better and had a little more self-confidence, I would never have dipped my toe into accountancy, but life can't be just about wonderful successes. You must make mistakes to grow.

- Working as a teacher at an underachieving comprehensive school in Leicester for 6 years was either a waste of time or an incredible learning experience depending upon which lens I look through. It showed me how **not** to run a school and gave me the freedom to try some things that I thought might make a difference to the lives of young people from underprivileged backgrounds. It isn't often in life that you are able to take such risks. There were moments during those 6 years when I really wondered what I was doing with my life but battling through the jungle was worthwhile.

- For three summers, I attended a University Summer School at which I learned more about leadership. It was quite a sacrifice as I had a family, and the 6-week summer holiday is precious to teachers. The school I was working at funded the experience so they must have seen that I had something to offer the world. I learned lots and earned a Master's in Educational Studies. Going the extra mile was increasingly important to me. I had discovered ambition.

- Applying for 20 Deputy Headteacher jobs, having 10 interviews, and regularly being rejected was demoralising but showed me the importance of resilience, of keeping going. Eventually I got a job in Nottingham working with Chris Archer, a man who I connected with. I nearly gave up. Thanks goodness I didn't.

- I was the Head of 3 very different secondary schools in the East Midlands. Each had its problems and I enjoyed helping to solve them. I was regularly praised and appreciated. Creating teams, motivating the staff and the students, promoting the schools, and raising achievement came naturally. I was in my element. I had found the ideal world for my skills. I know I did a good job at each of the schools. Eventually, I was persuaded to form a Multi-Academy Trust which included the school I was leading and 2 more that I had been asked to take on because they had serious problems. Trusts were new things. There weren't any real rules. It was a bit of a free for all. I was never comfortable as a CEO in that environment, even though I had loved being a Headteacher. Spreading myself across three schools and trying to move the Trust forward in such a confused world wasn't much fun. So, at 60, I stepped down to do other things.

- When I first entered the word of semi-retirement I felt let down. I knew that I had given others chances that they didn't seem to have appreciated, that some authorities- national and local- seemed keen to see me depart the scene because I had sometimes been critical, that peers had probably lobbied against me and damaged my reputation. I think such emotions are normal when you leave the stage. Some of the reaction might have been justified but I realised that there was nothing I could do to change any of it now. Given my time again I would have probably taken a few slightly different steps but all I could do was take the learning to my new situation and embrace the fresh reality. Stephen Covey wrote about paradigm shifts, about seeing the same situation in a different way. Instead of feeling badly treated, I decided to let go and see the new situation as a great opportunity to live a different type of life. That has turned out well.

- Since then I've cycled in France, India and Vietnam, chaired Football Association Disciplinary panels, written two books, helped spread good careers education across schools, coached people, become the Chair of a charity, tried playing golf and speaking better French, looked after a pony, hosted a podcast series, bought a campervan, joined a running group, become a Lay Advisor for the Criminal Justice System, acquired a spaniel and graduated to grandad status. I'm always keen to have new experiences and to keep learning. Climbing Mount Kilimanjaro was an amazing experience which taught me a lot.

I summarised my life in a few paragraphs to show that there have been times when I have struggled. I have felt alone. I have felt that I have been treated unfairly. I have felt that my talent had not been recognised. I have felt that I haven't had any talent. My dad died. My daughters have been sick. I spent time in hospital myself. I have been bullied at work. I have fallen out with friends. These things happen in life. I have stepped from Comfort Zones into Fear Zones on many occasions, sometimes voluntarily, and occasionally through circumstance. Like others I have tried to embrace what has been thrown and tried to emerge stronger. It isn't always easy but then as Dr Seuss said:

"Nobody said life would be easy, they just promised it would be worth it."

On the day that we attacked the summit of Mount Kilimanjaro, I experienced serious discomfort. Between midnight and 4.00am I had trudged along, step by step, following others in the darkness. From 4.00am, serious fatigue set in. The causes of this were numerous. I had barely slept for 4 days. I had walked 40 miles uphill. I was wearing too many clothes. The air was thin at 6,000m above sea level, I was a bit overweight. I was 63 ½ years old.

So many reasons for the discomfort. The four hours from 4.00am were so hard. Putting one foot in front of the other felt outrageously difficult. Marwa encouraged, cajoled, and pushed me to Stella Point and then to the Summit. When I got to Stella Point, the end of the steep climb, and the Summit became visible I said to Marwa "I can't go on" and his response will always stay with me "30 minutes of pain or 30 years of regret. The choice is yours".   The discomfort, the pain was worth it. It usually is.

I did experience genuine discomfort on the slopes of Kilimanjaro. In my personal life and in my career, I have sometimes felt scared and uncomfortable. There have been lots of setbacks but the older I have become the more I am aware of the importance of keeping going. Our friend Maslow said:

"One can choose to go back toward safety or forward toward growth. Growth must be chosen again and again; fear must be overcome again and again."

And if we experience failure, as I often have, we need to remember that most successful people have failed spectacularly. Don't believe me? Well….

- Thomas Edison eventually invented the light bulb but had failed with 10,000 previous attempts.

- Lady Gaga is a huge music star but she was let go by a record company which didn't think she had enough talent to make it.

- Stephen King is one of the world's best-selling writers, but his first novel "Carrie" was rejected by publishers 30 times.

- The basketball player Michael Jordan is one of the world's most famous sports stars, but he has clear memories of not being picked for his High School team and crying in his bedroom. He also tells the story of 26 times missing a shot that would have won a game.

- Elvis Presley is probably the most famous pop star of all time and yet he was told early in his career "You ain't goin' nowhere son. You ought to go back to driving a truck".

- Elizabeth Arden founded an amazingly successful cosmetics and beauty salon business but had previously failed as a nurse, a bank clerk, and a receptionist.

- And my favourite one is Walt Disney. The person who founded the Disney Corporation with cartoons such as Donald Duck, theme parks like Disneyland and films such as Dumbo, Aladdin and Beauty and the Beast was sacked by a magazine because, wait for it, he wasn't creative enough!

7 stories that illustrate the need to keep going through the Fear Zone. It is so easy to retreat to what you know you can do and accept the criticism

of others. The discomfort isn't usually physical, it more usually manifests itself as mental pain. The one certainty is that if you cave in after one or two negative comments or experiences, you will not grow and will be destined to stay in that lovely, cuddly but probably eventually gloomy Comfort Zone. I have done it too often and the backward steps still haunt me. In the examples I gave earlier, if I had not hacked through the Fear Zone I would probably never have gone to university, never have become a teacher- and certainly never a Headteacher, never have met my wife or seen my family develop around me and would probably be living the type of life that the writer Thoreau described as *'quiet desperation'*. Giving in to the discomfort of Kilimanjaro's final slope would have been a huge regret, I thank Marwa for making me persevere.

Footnote to this section.

It would be remiss of me to omit my experience of being seriously ill in 1992. I had suffered from Hepatitis A over the Christmas break. That wasn't pleasant. The doctor told me to take 2 weeks off work and when I returned I was feeling good. So, I started to ride my bike to work and even began jogging. Within 5 days I felt a tingling in my fingers and toes. I was becoming weaker. My hands and feet had abnormal sensation. I could barely hold a pen and walking was becoming difficult. I visited the GP who assured me it was a "minor neuropathy" that would clear up in a week or so. But it didn't. It got worse. A friend of mine was dating a medical student and when he told her my symptoms she immediately said "It sounds like Guillain Barre Syndrome. Tell him to book an appointment with Mr. Critchley." I did, and it was.

Mr. Critchley arranged for an immediate admission to hospital where I experienced a variety of tests including a lumbar puncture and electrical tests to gauge conductivity of my nerves. I was there for 4 days and was surrounded by men who were experiencing treatment for brain tumours, strokes, and undiagnosed ailments. It was explained to me that my too rapid return to exertion had fooled my immune system into action on the understanding that there was something wrong with me again. It had fought off the Hepatitis and now it had another battle. But of course, there was nothing there and so it attacked my nervous system making it incapable of sending messages to my limbs. I left the hospital in a wheelchair. It was very worrying.

We had 2 small children by this stage. Anne had three people to look after. Her parents were parachuted in from Ireland. Slowly- very slowly- I got better. I visited a physiotherapist who helped the recovery. At one stage she was thinking of sending me to a residential recovery centre in Warwickshire but decided I was motivated enough to follow a solo programme. Step ups on the stairs, squeezing a foam ball and practicing handwriting progressed to walking upstairs, lifting tins of beans above my head and walks around the garden. Within 3 months I was ready for a phased return to work. 6 months after admission to hospital I played a game of football.

Since then, the word "discomfort" has taken on a different dimension. Guillain Barre Syndrome took me to a new place. I was genuinely scared that I would never be the same again. I have lived with a slight tingling in the soles of my feet but beyond that I recovered fully. I'm not sure that the other people on the Ward did. It made me wary of saying that anything that has followed was worth getting agitated about. Feeling very tired on a mountain slope in Africa? A minor inconvenience!

If you would like to find out more about discomfort, check out the "I DID YOU CAN" interview with Jack Buckner then CEO of British Swimming – and now in the same role at UK Athletics. Jack was a top athlete. He won the Gold medal at the 1986 European Championships in the 5000 metres and represented the UK in 2 Olympic Games. Sport has been Jack's life. He would have loved to have been a top cricketer, but it was at running that he excelled. Training and competing were everything to him but eventually injuries and the need for money to support his family meant he had to step away. And his business career moved along at quite a pace too. It proved to be a more than adequate replacement for athletics and he quickly rose through the ranks of the corporate giant Adidas. But it was then that discomfort appeared on the scene.

The demands placed on an Executive with a major company meant that he was barely seeing his family. He saw his children far less than he wanted to and sat down to discuss the situation with his then wife. They agreed to make a change. And it was a massive change. Jack resigned from his high-flying post with Adidas and left the west coast of the USA in pursuit of a new dream. He bought an apple orchard in New Zealand. Jack describes the move as a "disaster". When asked why he decided to buy the orchard he refers to the culture that he was absorbed in. Americans encouraged him to chase his dream and the shared understanding was that "hey, we can do anything if we put our mind to it". Making the orchard work was not something Jack could do. The decision brought great discomfort and when he sold up, he lost a lot of money - as well as finding himself without a job.

He returned to the UK and managed to find some work through contacts in the sporting world, but it wasn't really satisfying, and he had 5 quite barren years before he was appointed to a permanent role in Sport England- and from there things took off again. He was soon the CEO at British Triathlon and then became the boss of British Swimming. Since our interview he has returned, with a certain inevitability, to lead UK Athletics.

Jack looks back without regret but acknowledges the pain that he experienced when his post athletics career went wrong. He has always been blessed with an optimistic and enthusiastic nature and sees the "wasted years" as a resting period which has prepared him to carry on working when friends and colleagues have retired. Jack is still raring to go.

Scan to hear the full interview with Jack.

My Kilimanjaro tips for expecting discomfort and battling through it are:

- You are not the first person to experience discomfort. Keep going. Some people manage to create an illusion of perpetual tranquillity. The swan moving smoothly across the lake is of course propelled by frantically moving legs which hide beneath the surface.

- Visualise how you will feel if you give in and how you will feel if you get there? When you do get there, look back at how you would have felt if you had given up. It might not be a positive sensation, but it could give you extra energy for the next challenge – and the associated discomfort- that you will face.

- These are always difficult times when you are trying to accomplish something. If it was easy perhaps it wouldn't be worthwhile. There will be better moments ahead and the feeling of satisfaction will be so uplifting. Life changing in many cases.

Life lesson 7: Work hard

"The only place where success comes before work is in the dictionary."

Vidal Sassoon: Hairdresser and entrepreneur

Some of the guides and porters had climbed Mount Kilimanjaro more than 200 times. That is seriously hard work. The work involved carrying tents, luggage, and food-even toilets-up a steep hill, often in bleak weather. It involved sleeping in a tent with perhaps 10 others. It involved serious responsibility. Travellers had paid a lot of money for their experience and assumed competence and care from the guides. It appears that almost always they got it. The paying punters in our team had immense respect for the hard work of the G Adventures staff that we climbed with.

Jackson told me that he was learning to speak a 4th language to further his career. He aimed to become a safari guide. Others did not see that as a possibility and would continue to porter and support. If they stopped working hard the chances were that future work would not emerge. There were plenty of people willing to take their place.

It was admirable and, as I lay awake at night, I pondered the times that I had worked extremely hard in my life and how it had paid a dividend. Sometimes hard work feels imposed. You are told to do it and it is resented. In my brief sojourn as a trainee accountant, I was instructed to sit in the attic of a shipbuilding company in East Anglia hunting for specific invoices and wage slips for hours on end. I am sure there was a reason for it, but it was never fully explained to me and it felt pointless, a waste of my time. However, when I was preparing lessons as a geography teacher, time ceased to exist. I could spend hour after hour building upon ideas and creating new resources. It made sense to me. I was a little less enthusiastic about the marking though.

When I was a headteacher I would leave home at 6.45am and drive 30 miles up the M1 to work in a pressurised environment. Meetings with inspectors, assemblies, meetings with parents, meeting with members of staff, writing letters, preparing policies, occasionally teaching, dealing with pupils who had misbehaved, planning improvements to the building. All this would be packed into the time before 6.00pm and then there might be governors' meetings, parent events or presentation evenings. There was rarely a quiet moment. And I loved it. Hard work was a way of life.

When I made it home, I had three daughters to take to swimming and music lessons, read stories to and perhaps even watch a bit of TV with. And when they had gone to bed I would plan for the next day. At weekends I would run, take the girls to events, visit relatives.... and maybe mark a set of books. A visit to a football match was a major bonus. I was always busy. Always working hard. I was in my element. Rarely did I resent the invasion of work into my time. I was not alone. Anne worked super hard. We have discussed these times with our daughters, and they feel that they didn't miss out on life. They did everything they wanted to do and appreciate the energy it must have taken. It appears they are taking the same approach with their own families.

Working hard can be exhilarating, almost addictive. It is fine when you feel that it is making a difference. Less good when it seems you are just filling time. There needs to be a purpose. There needs to be some sort of balance. In the education world I was able to take my foot off the accelerator during the school holidays. Not everyone has that bonus of course.

As part of the **"I DID YOU CAN"** podcast series I interviewed Alix Manning-Jones who has a key role in helping young people from Derby overcome socio-economic disadvantage. Alix told me about her life as a busy woman, married to a busy plumber with a young daughter and a disabled mother who requires care- and a puppy that demands attention. Alix packs meetings, interviews and paperwork into her working schedule as well having a hectic domestic life. She thrives upon the hard work.

Alix was brought up in a single parent family, had no positive role models and at 14 saw little hope. However, after joining an Arts group, she became absorbed by performance. She spent so much time with other young people who loved the Arts. Time almost ceased to exist, so engrossed were they in what they were doing. Later she was to be offered a paid internship with the Royal Shakespeare Company and her eyes opened even wider to the excitement of work in a world that suited her.

She currently works in a different world, inspiring young people from troubled backgrounds to try to fulfil their potential. The habit of hard work that she took from those teenage experiences has stayed with her. Different world, same passion, impressive results.

I have already mentioned Malcolm Gladwell's suggestion that it takes 10,000 hours to master a skill. I think it is fair to say that some sign of talent must exist if someone is to truly excel. I have tried to play golf. It would take me 10,000 hours of practice to get around an 18-hole course with my dignity intact let alone challenge to win a tournament. The violinist Isaac Stern was once introduced to a woman who said, "I would give my life to play like that" and he responded with "Lady, that I did." Perhaps he could have shown a little more grace, but it does seem like an accurate description of the time he had devoted to reaching the level he was at i.e. probably the best violinist in the world.

I have long had an interest in cycle racing. It has struck me as a sort of chess on wheels, but it's a game of chess that takes them over the highest mountains and insists that they cover up to 200 kilometres in a day. That is frighteningly hard work. I suggest sceptics have a look at the Tour de France when it is on TV in July. I have witnessed a few stages in the major tours. I have no idea how they do it. Extraordinary. The training that goes unseen is breathtaking.

In his book "My Time" (2012) Tour de France and Olympic champion Bradley Wiggins describes some of the work he had to do to be in peak condition for the challenges he faced in the summer of 2012.

"The goal in the plan was to do 100,000m of climbing between March and June. If you work it out it was about 10,000m a week- a little bit more than going from sea level to the top of Everest."

Cyclists are showing this sort of commitment throughout the year and, of course, most don't win. They keep working very, very hard regardless.

It isn't just sport that requires hard work if someone is to give of their best. The hours that go into preparing for a major performance in a West End play can only be imagined by most of us. The great literary works do not emerge from an afternoon's activity. J. K. Rowling had the idea for "Harry Potter and the Philosopher's Stone" in 1991 but didn't complete it until 1995, and it was only published in 1997. Arguably the most famous sculpture in the world is Michaelangelo's "David". 3 years of total commitment were needed to ensure the finished item was exactly what the sculptor wanted to create and 500 years later visitors still admire it in Florence's Gallarea dell Academia.

The artist Salvador Dali once said:

"No masterpiece was ever painted by a lazy artist."

And I think that sums it up. If you are half hearted about something it will become apparent quite quickly. Questions will be asked about your commitment. What you create will disappoint.

Whilst hard work matters there is no suggestion that you should not have time to do other things beyond your paid work. Managing your time is important. Most of us are likely to be in paid employment of some sort for 30 years or more. In so many jobs the number of tasks to be completed can be overwhelming. They need to be managed thoughtfully.

There are many time management techniques in use today. It is worth considering a few of them.

1.Parkinson's Law

The historian Cyril Parkinson became famous for his phrase *"work expands so as to fill the time available for its completion."* In other words, the amount of time you give yourself to complete a specific task is the amount of time it will take you to complete that task. And that so often seems to be the case. Parkinson argued that we often assign too much time to a task and that holds up progress.

Once you understand this it is amazing how much you can get done in an hour, a day, a week, a year. To implement your new learning it is worth working in bursts. Try working without a computer charger, assign an amount of time to a task and then cut it in half and see if you can still do it. Drastically reduce the amount of time you allocate to 'chewing gum' activities such as checking Instagram or scrolling through Twitter (X). It's amazing how much time can be freed up.

2.The Pareto Principle

The 80/20 rule is an idea created of the Italian economist Vilfredo Pareto. It's the view that 20% of actions are responsible for 80% of outcomes. The goal of Pareto analysis is to help you prioritize tasks that are most effective at solving problems. You can do a lot of work and it makes little difference so give early thought as to which actions will pay the biggest dividend.

A way of approaching this is: -

1. List some of the problems you are facing.
2. Identify the cause of each problem.
3. Give a score to each problem.
4. Group the problems together according to their cause.
5. Add up the score of each group- and the group with the highest score is the issue you should work on first.

3.The Eisenhower Matrix

Dwight Eisenhower became President of the USA in 1953. Before that he had been an Allied Forces Commander during the Second World War. Every day he had to deal with difficult decisions, and he came up with a device that helped him to prioritise what he should do.

He decided it was best to place your tasks / decisions into four separate quadrants. He decided it was best to place your tasks into one of 4 quadrants (see below) which related to their relative importance and urgency. Urgent tasks are those he felt needed to be done immediately. Important tasks are those that make a difference to long term goals. Eisenhower believed you should only work on tasks in the top two quadrants—the other tasks, you should delete or delegate. Which is, of course, fine if you have someone to delegate to!

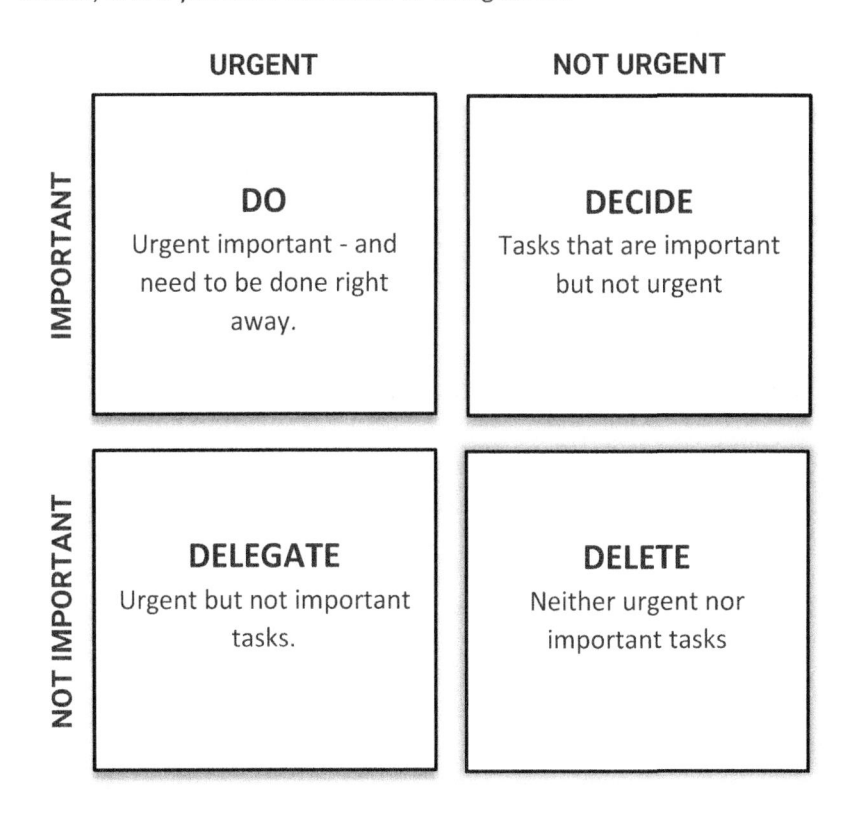

	URGENT	**NOT URGENT**
IMPORTANT	**DO** — Urgent important - and need to be done right away.	**DECIDE** — Tasks that are important but not urgent
NOT IMPORTANT	**DELEGATE** — Urgent but not important tasks.	**DELETE** — Neither urgent nor important tasks

It is interesting to consider where you place different tasks or actions. There are not necessarily right or wrong answers but have a look at the list below and place them in one of the boxes.

Analyse data for a report due next month ……..Go to the gym……….Write a report for your manager about a disciplinary issue you witnessed yesterday ………..Return a call from your mother (it's rare that she calls) ………. Check social media………… Call a lawyer about a case that is in court later in the week………….. Call IT support to ask them to fix your computer……. Write an application for a job………. Organise a training day that is planned for next week…….. Call the Agency to arrange secretarial cover for a colleague……. Book your flight to Ibiza…Tidy your drawer……Attend a meeting about next year's schedule.

So much depends upon the context …….. but I would recommend you call your mother first. It will nag away at you. It might be something important, it might not but if it's on your mind it's unlikely you will be at your best. I'd also say social media probably doesn't need to be checked for a while. Unless checking social media is your job of course!

It worked for President Eisenhower. So, try it out.

4.The Jam Jar model.

Picture your day as an empty jam jar. You have a range of actions that need to be done. How will you fit them in? This model suggests you classify them as:

Sand: Phone calls, text messages and emails fall into this category. If they aren't done today, it won't make any difference.

Pebbles: These are tasks that need to be done but necessarily today – and not by you.

Rocks: These are important. You **have to** deal with them.

So, you put the rocks into the jar first, then fit a few pebbles in and then if there's any space the sand can fill it up. It's worth a go.

The central point that links each of the 4 systems/techniques/ideas is that you need to take care of your time. You have a life to lead. Friends to keep in touch with, relationships to nurture, homes to maintain, meals to cook and fitness to consider. Work matters and working hard will make a difference. For short periods of time, you may need to be obsessed but a racehorse that never gets a rest is unlikely to run, let alone win, many races.

During my time on Kilimanjaro, I saw plenty of evidence that hard work matters and is appreciated. I also noted that "rest and relaxation" has its place too.

If you would like to find out more about working hard check out my interview with Steve Hughes on "I DID YOU CAN". *Steve describes himself as someone who finds buyers for IT companies. He has built a career upon immersing himself in companies who have not yet reached their potential, working hard to make them profitable, finding a buyer…….. and making himself redundant. It's a formula that has been working for 30 years and has helped him create a very enjoyable life. He has recently expanded into the music industry by founding a record label and recording studio and helping acts to maximise their potential.*

Steve spent his early years in Toxteth, one of the more deprived parts of Liverpool. When he was nine his parents and his three siblings went to live in Ashton-in-Makerfield, a small town about 25 miles to the east of the city. They lived in a 2 up 2 down terraced house and, whilst life was comfortable, Steve did not have access to any entrepreneurial wizards.

In his early years Steve lacked confidence in himself. There were few hints that he would be a success in the commercial world. He liked school and did well enough in the sciences to earn a place studying biology at the John Moores University. However, he was never destined to use the biological knowledge he acquired because he was recruited by the Manchester-based National Computer Centre and threw himself into the emerging world of computers. He quickly acquired skills which put him ahead of the vast majority of striving young professionals. As computers developed so did Steve.

He worked out that there was a certain amount of volatility in the computer world and that firms came and went. Steve worked exceptionally hard to turn a company around and was identified as someone who could make an impact. He says that looking back he recognises that he was obsessed by the projects he engaged with and is of the view that there are times when obsession is needed to really do justice to yourself and your work.

Steve's hard work has brought significant financial reward. He has even been able to take years off to travel and spend time with his family. At the moment, he is obsessed by his music business and a new job leading a company carved out from another and intends making both a success. In parallel, Steve is a Board Advisor at a new USA-based start-up and Chairman of a UK-based electricity supplier. His view is that very hard work earns rewards and that such commitment is essential if potential is to be fulfilled.

Scan to hear the full interview with Steve.

My Kilimanjaro tips about working hard are:

- Occasionally you may need to be obsessed by a task. It might completely take over your life. For a short period, this can be appropriate. It can transform the goal you are working towards. But you can't carry on like that forever.

- Consider carefully what you need to get done and prioritise. The Important and Urgent things need to get done even if it involves working beyond your scheduled day. If you leave them incomplete it will annoy those you are working with- and you - because if you have managed to read as far as this, you are clearly determined to make a positive impact.

- If you get a reputation for working hard it will take you a long way in life. It will endear you to others and almost inevitably, you will achieve more. It will also give you immense satisfaction. Twiddling your thumbs is not a healthy way to spend your day.

- If your mother calls out of the blue, make sure you take the call. If you don't it will play on your mind, and you will not do your best work. Of course, the call might only be to remind you to buy your aunt a present for her 25th wedding anniversary – but it might not be!

Life lesson 8: Consider leadership.

"If your actions inspire people to dream more, learn more and become more, you are a leader "

John Quincy Jones

Emmanuel was an excellent leader. He had a role that would make many of us flinch. First of all, he had responsibility for 10 people from across the world who had paid a lot of money to be part of the expedition to climb Kilimanjaro. I was the old feller at 63. Iggy was the youngster at 24. Emmanuel had to create an environment in which we were given the opportunity to gel as a team and to enjoy the experience. He also had to give us all the best possible chance to get to the top of the mountain without jeopardising our health. And all this was to be done through his second language. Quite a challenge.

But there was more. He also had to lead a team of 20 porters which had been pulled together for this trip. Whilst some of them knew each other, most didn't. They had been recruited by others for Emmanuel to work with. I knew little about the politics of recruiting from different tribes, but I was told that it was not always easy to get individuals to work across tribal boundaries. It is also fair to say that the range of responsibilities was extraordinary. How does a leader create a world in which those who are emptying toilets, collecting water from springs, and carrying luggage on heads feel at ease with those who were making decisions about routes, tourist wellbeing and the daily menus?

Every day Emmanuel addressed the multi-national group with confidence. He kept us informed, smiled when appropriate and intervened if he saw a risk to wellbeing. At the same time, he oversaw the support team with a quiet authority. He ensured that they all introduced themselves at the end of their dance/singing performance on Monday afternoon and there was no sign of anyone slipping in the standard of work. It might be that the porters knew that future employment would be dependent upon Emmanuel speaking positively about them. It certainly seemed that there were more applicants for posts than there were jobs available.

There were times when Emmanuel showed that he did not know his team as well as he would have liked. This was most notable when we left our tents at midnight, and he told us that the porters not accompanying us on the final climb would be occupying our tents for security reasons. This was followed by a suggestion that we take valuables with us. Presumably he suspected that one or two of his team might be tempted by any cash, cards or cameras that were left in the tents.

As I said in the debrief:

"Emmanuel is an excellent leader. He knew how to motivate his team and his clients. The expedition went very smoothly. Without him it would not have felt as enjoyable."

My leadership experience.

Leadership matters. I enjoyed leading. I look back to my childhood and remember assembling a village football team to play against Downall Green when I was 11. My first recollection of being a leader was when I answered the door to see 2 boys who I didn't know. They were called Neil and Clive. They were brothers. Neil was younger and Clive was deaf. Neil asked if I would let them play for "your football team.". It was mine? Who knew?

During my school days, opportunities for leadership were few. I lacked the confidence to put myself in a position to lead anything. I just followed. It was the same for much of my university life. I didn't really think I was in a position to make decisions which affected others. Upon reflection it must have been annoying for others. "Which pub shall we go to?" someone might ask. "I don't mind" I would respond. It's fine to be easy going but to constantly expect others to make the decisions is surely lazy. I referred earlier to the question "Are you a dolphin or a bottle?". I was certainly a bottle in those days but with an underlying urge to be a dolphin. I just lacked the confidence.

Being asked to first captain and then manage the football team that I joined in my early 20's was so significant. I found that I enjoyed taking responsibility for team selection, recruitment of new players, training, tactics (they were limited. I was more Ted Lasso than Pep Guardiola) and motivation. It all felt natural even though some of the team members were a lot older than me. As I grew into it, I found that I also enjoyed dealing with the club finances, the bar rota, and discussions with the league authorities. I was feeling like I made a difference. It was from this experience in my mid 20's that I started to find ambition at work. I looked at the way I was led and increasingly despaired. I knew that if I was to stay in teaching for 30 years or more, I would have to be a decision maker, a leader.

My first leadership role at work came when I became responsible for twenty 15-year-olds who had been identified as "unlikely to succeed in examinations". Effectively the school system had written them off and I was to entertain them for 70% of their time in school for 2 years. There wasn't a queue of people ready to take on the role. It was such a mixed bag. There were Brendon and Ben- big lads who just didn't see the point of school. Julian was artistic and coming to terms with his sexuality (this was England in the 80's), Alison and Maria – both scared of their own shadows, Tracy – larger than life in so many ways. What a cast.

One of the pupils was called David. I met him again 10 years ago as I was waiting to see "The King and I" at a theatre in Leicester. He introduced me to his wife and said, "This is the only teacher who realised I was dyslexic and tried to teach me in a different way." I remembered David as a superb artist. Dyslexia wasn't much discussed in those days but looking back I can now see that he had all the symptoms. I was so pleased that he spoke to me. He looked happy and healthy. Perhaps the educational diet of visits, visitors, drama, art, general knowledge quizzes, reading and writing that I organised had worked.

I devote a paragraph to that first taste of leadership in the workplace because it ignited a flame. I saw that I could make decisions that made lives better, including my own. It was far from a perfect two years but as I reflect, I can see how I grew.

When I was 30, I wrote down my ambition to be a Deputy Headteacher by the time I was 37 and a Headteacher by the time I was 40. I achieved both goals and enjoyed being in charge from the off. I just knew what to do. Obviously, I got some things wrong but in a five-year period we moved the school from risk of closure with poor examination results, bad behaviour, low staff morale and ever decreasing pupil numbers to one that inspectors praised. I was described as "inspirational". Was there ever a better tribute? From there, I was asked to take over another school that was badly bruised and applied the same ideas that I had used at my first post: --

1. Introduce myself with confidence and share a little information about my life.

2. Present an early vision of what the school will become.

3. Ask the staff to tell me their views about what works well and what needs to be improved. Analyse the results and share them. It's "We" not "Me".

4. Lead weekly briefings with confidence, a smile- and congratulations when earned. But address concerns if necessary.

5. Don't hide in my office.

6. Build a senior team that knew what it was doing. A clear grid that showed who did what. No hiding places.

My mate Fran told me that the French film director Francois Truffaut once said:

"Everyone has one great film in them, but the trouble is we keep repeating it over and over again." (I must confess that I can find no record of this, so if it was someone else who first said it, I apologise and hope we can settle out of court).

I suspect it is true of me. The formula that I employed worked in my first leadership role and the second. So why would I not use it in other schools that I was asked to lead?

I have seen football managers adopt the same basic technique at their different clubs. Sometimes it's appropriate but occasionally it isn't. Jose Mourinho is perhaps the best example of this. It worked at Chelsea and didn't at Tottenham.

The need for leadership

Leaders have very different styles. I was an admirer of the long-standing German Chancellor Angela Merkel. She emerged from a relatively poor background in East Germany and led the government of the united country from 2005 to 2021. I can only imagine the pressure that she experienced during that period. There must have been many ambitious colleagues keen to take her place, quite apart from the official opposition parties who would look to criticise her decisions. Merkel was perhaps at her most commanding when she bravely committed Germany to admitting more Syrian refugees than other European countries. Part of this was because of human decency but she could also see that Germany would need workers over the next decade and that the migrants could match that need. In the following few years there were some terrorist attacks in Germany and her approach to the migrant crisis seemed to damage her popularity. She stepped down in 2021 with an extraordinary legacy and must have thought about the former American First Lady Eleanor Roosevelt's words:

"Do what you feel in your heart to be right- for you'll be criticised anyway."

Other leaders emerge in very different circumstances. Nemonte Nenquimo is an Ecuadorian woman in her 30's who has taken on oil companies and her government on behalf of the Waorani people. It must take remarkable courage to go eyeball to eyeball with powerful and unscrupulous organisations but as the environment of her country faces annual diminishment, it seems she took the view *"If not me, then who?"*- a line used very effectively by the actor Heather Watson when she spoke about women's rights so eloquently at the United Nations.

Over the last couple of months, there has rightly been much discussion about the Good Friday Agreement which brought peace to Northern Ireland in 1998. There had been almost 30 years of violence on the streets, and it seemed that there would never be a shared understanding of how peace could be delivered. It was quite amazing that the Governments of Ireland and the UK, assisted by that of the USA, managed to work with the communities of Northern Ireland to bring a new calmness. Leaders had been talking and co-operating for some time and many of them could take some of the plaudits. Tony Blair and Bertie Ahearn were Prime Ministers of the two governments, John Hulme and

David Trimble emerged as leaders of the two distinct Republican and Unionist communities, whilst Martin McGuinness and Ian Paisley persuaded the more violent elements to give peace a chance. The British Secretary of State Mo Mowlam famously worked through cancer treatment to overcome hurdles that the Agreement faced. Mairead Corrigan and Betty Williams had earlier been awarded the Nobel Prize for Peace for their work in trying to broker peace. Monica McWilliams and Bronagh Hinds had more recently founded the Northern Ireland Women's Coalition. All these people played a role in bringing peace to Northern Ireland. All led in their own way. Without them it wouldn't have happened.

If you have an instinctive feeling that you could lead, then 'Just Do It' (Thanks Nike) is my advice. To avoid it will lead to certain frustration. If you lead, you will certainly have frustrating moments but the overriding feeling of being in charge of your own destiny will help enormously. You don't have to do anything remarkable. Just doing something that needs doing is leadership. Remember *"If not me then who?"*

On the slopes of Kilimanjaro, I saw Emmanuel being a role model. Younger people were looking at him and thinking "I would like to do that" and sometimes, I imagine, "That's easy, why can't I be given the chance to do that?". In years to come, others will look back on their lives and see him as an influence. He showed them what was possible. I hope I did the same to some small extent. I once thought about how many people that I had led who had moved on to become headteachers. I counted 10. That's pretty good going. Some would have done it without me, some were given chances by me that others might not have given them, and some probably thought "If he can do that, I'm sure I can". Fair enough. We are all motivated in different ways.

I conclude this section with a quote that I have always liked from American business guru Warren Bennis I don't want to waste it.

> *"Becoming a leader is synonymous with becoming yourself. It is precisely that simple and it is also that difficult."*

If you would like to find out more about leadership, please listen to my interview with Sue Churchill as part of the "I DID YOU CAN" podcast series. Sue Churchill is an architect. I met her when we commissioned her company to design a new Sixth Form Centre at a school I was leading. She always wanted to be an architect. At the age of 26 she became co-owner of an architectural practice, and it continues to thrive. That sounds so straightforward, doesn't it? But it can't have been. Sue has succeeded in what has been very much a male dominated world.

Sue was brought up in Stroud in Gloucestershire. Her home life was a little different to others in that she did not watch TV until she was a teenager and classical music was played every day. The family holidayed in a touring caravan. There were no overseas trips. There were no architects in her family, but Sue knew from the age of 10 that she wanted to design buildings. There was never a doubt in her mind. She wonders if conversations with her father- an engineer- as they walked around her hometown looking at buildings might have been a factor in her early choice of career. Sue did well at the all-girls school that she attended, the focus on examinations suited her, and she earned a place at Nottingham University to study…… architecture. Who would have guessed?

Sue was absorbed by her course and after 7 years she was a fully qualified architect. Within 2 years she was the co-owner of a practice. This was remarkable. A young woman at the forefront of a business in the building world. It just didn't happen. And it went well. The business eventually employed 65 people and worked on some exciting projects. Circumstances changed and Sue managed a re-structure that left her with 20 employees.

I enjoyed the conversation with Sue because she is leading in an area that she is passionate about. Her work is her pleasure. She sees architecture as a vocation. On holiday she checks out buildings. She especially enjoyed a recent trip to Berlin. She is planning to transform her own home into a truly eco-friendly building and always has an eye as to how architecture can contribute to moving the world closer to a carbon neutral world.

Alongside this continued excitement for her calling runs a deep understanding of what it means to lead. She has taken many decisions that have changed lives and is aware of the need to change direction when it is necessary. She wasn't taught to be a business leader as part of her university course but is now modestly confident - though happy to accept that she is learning every day about how to lead in an ever-changing world.

Scan for the full interview with Sue.

My Kilimanjaro tips about leadership are:

- The world needs leaders so why not you? All leaders were once not leaders. In some cases, it might have been better for the world if they had not found a taste for leadership. There are so many people who have the ability and knowledge but not the confidence to lead and the world can be the worse for their reluctance.

- The best leaders listen to other views before deciding. If you want an idea to be introduced successfully it is as well if as many people as possible know why a change in practice is needed so listening and explaining become key tools in the best leaders' bags.

- Succession plans are important for the organisation. Create pathways so that others can become leaders too. Give responsibility to others. This makes sense for the workload of the leader but also for the balance of the company/school/ university/ ship.

Some closing words.

The ascent of Mount Kilimanjaro was an opportunity for me to do something that I never thought I would do. Climbing the highest mountain in Africa never occurred to me as a possibility when I was growing up in Lancashire. Similarly becoming a Headteacher never seemed likely when I looked to the future. It is impossible for most people to predict their future life with any confidence. So many underestimate what they are capable of because they don't have the role models nor the platform to build upon.

When I was leading schools, I would stand in front of groups of children and tell them how excited they should be. Excited about what their futures held. Nobody knew what lay ahead. I would tell them that in the audience I had future nurses, dentists, plumbers, entrepreneurs, entertainers, builders, amazing parents, hairdressers, teachers, bankers, sports stars, lawyers, TV presenters……. I would look at individuals and ask what they thought they would be. I didn't expect a response. It was pure performance. There was so much potential in each audience. Some would be fulfilled, some wouldn't. Just imagine if everyone did what they were capable of doing? The conversations I made use of to create **"In Search of My Alumni"** suggested that the work done by schools to open the eyes of young people to their own potential was often limited due to examination and inspector pressures.

I started the podcast series **"I DID YOU CAN"** because I wanted to keep sharing the idea that human beings have different things to offer and by following their dreams they find satisfaction. I interviewed my old schoolmate Paul Harris who became a choreographer, my university friend Jan Wilkinson who led university libraries, an ex-colleague Ivan Palmer who taught in Vietnam and now Taiwan, Sue Churchill who is an architect, Jack Buckner the CEO of UK Athletics, Ruth Taylor – an accountant, Phil Gibbs- a barrister, Lewis Smith is an equine vet, Claire Linton a transport strategist and many more. **"I DID YOU CAN"** was an important project for me and I hope **"I Climbed Kilimanjaro"** builds upon it by illustrating what we can do when we have the confidence and the opportunity to push ourselves. Usually, we have to make the opportunity. It rarely just pops up.

Please believe me when I say I do not pretend to have done anything remarkable with my life. Climbing Kilimanjaro and leading schools would hardly be a footnote in some life stories. Many have done quite extraordinary things. Edmund Hillary, Tensing Norgay, Marie Curie, Roger Bannister, Amelia Earhart, Gertrude Ederle, and Ellen MacArthur were names that I mentioned earlier as people who had known what they wanted to achieve, prepared to get there, challenged themselves, networked, worked with others, dealt with serious discomfort, and taken the lead. Each stand out from the crowd because they took risks and changed the world just a little.

The participants in **"I DID YOU CAN"** are people I actually know. Please listen to them and create your own stories. Whatever your age or background.

As I lay sleeplessly on my mat in a small tent on the side of Mount Kilimanjaro, I thought about my own life. It has gone well. But I know I've got more to offer. However, not as much as the millions of people who follow. I hope that having read **"I Climbed Kilimanjaro"**, you will find ways to increase the satisfaction you derive from your life and also help others to become the people they are capable of being.

And the 8 Lessons from Kilimanjaro that I hope we can all share are: -

1. Know yourself

2. Prepare

3. Challenge yourself to do great things

4. Network- nicely

5. Be a good team player

6. Expect discomfort and battle through it

7. Work hard

8. Consider leadership

Good luck!

With thanks to:

Marwa for making me believe- and steering me away from "30 years of regret".

Emmanuel for his admirable leadership.

Ian from Dublin via Quorn for persuading me to join him on Kilimanjaro 2023.

Emma and Dan from Nuremberg (via Surrey and Leicestershire) for flagging up the opportunity.

Laura from Wexford, Laura, Sophie and Vicky from Melbourne, Iggy from Norway, and Chad from Ohio for being such a supportive and entertaining group.

The Doc from Dar es Salaam.

'Suella' from Moshi via North London.

Al from Crumlin.

The people I met as I toured England to research "In Search of My Alumni".

The people I interviewed as part of the " I DID YOU CAN" podcast series: John Fallon, Gerry MacNamee, Alix Manning-Jones, Alex Bulman, Amy Mitchell, Etienne Stott, Donna Warren, Debbie Stanley, Marcus Jones, Sak Rafique, Pete Bell, Sarah Phillips, Dean Ratcliffe, Jessica Faulkner, Ivan Palmer, Matt Raine, Ross Crombie, Paul Harris, Jenny McConnell, David Dike, Liam Lambert, Tina Byrom, Sue Churchill, Jan Wilkinson, Gary Toward, Claire Knee, Eric Greenhalgh, Ian Gregson, Becky Valentine, Rob Pittam, Laura Grant, Steve Hughes, Tim Garratt, Syd Samuels, Sarah Naylor, Nick Butler, Liz Slingsby, John Johnson, Frasier Williamson, Jay Sandhu, John Dabrowski, Jack Buckner, Rachel Morris, David Hughes,

James Hall, Alice Gregson, Neil Timms, Sonia Byers, Naomi Burton, Peter Gates, Gemma Myles, Peter Carlisle, Jacqui Callan, Phil Gibbs, Ruth Taylor, Lewis Smith.

All the interviews can be accessed by scanning.............

Mark Oldham and David Knights for patiently checking the text.

Don Hale and Steve Green for helping to make the book a reality.

Cat, Maire, and Siobhan for steering me in the right direction.

And especially Anne for somehow managing the family, the house and Milo the spaniel whilst I was in Africa XX

The Author

Philip Crompton was brought up near Wigan in Lancashire but taught and led schools across the East Midlands for 36 years before embracing a portfolio lifestyle that includes writing, coaching, consultancy, public speaking, and travel.

His previous publications include:

"In Search of My Alumni" (2019) published by John Catt Educational.

"We All Ride Bikes Now" with Joanna Ward (2020) published by Four Winds

Philip also presents the podcast series "I DID YOU CAN" -accessed through Spotify.

He lives in Nottinghamshire and sometimes uses X (Twitter) as @PhilCrompton3.

Printed in Great Britain
by Amazon